You Are the Blue Sky
Understanding who you are beyond your thinking

"A beautifully personal sharing of the impact of knowing who you are and how perfectly well you are made."

~ **Michael Neill,** international bestselling author of *The Inside-Out Revolution* and *The Space Within*

"In *You Are the Blue Sky* Sarah Kostin has written a poetic and touchingly personal book of her own journey of awakening. Her writing is so sweet and powerful that we take that journey right along with her. I'm buying copies for friends, family and clients and I predict you will do the same."

~ **Steve Chandler,** author of *Time Warrior*

"This beautiful book is a simple, profound, and hopeful exploration of how we can connect more powerfully to our true nature. Through personal insights and the stories of others, Sarah helps us see the gift running through all of life and shows us how to find ourselves and our wisdom amongst it all, even when it seems far away."

~ **Barbara Patterson,** international coach & consultant

"A book full of love, wit and profound sharings of what it is to be human, and how easy it is for us to forget. Sarah Kostin's *You are The Blue Sky* is a beautiful blend of her own personal (often amusing) insights and seeing that what is true for her is true for all of us. Easy and enjoyable to read, this is already very high on my 'recommend to others' list."

~ **Wyn Morgan,** certified Master Transformative Coach and Corporate Change Agent

"This book is a gift of love. Sarah Kostin speaks deeply, bravely, compassionately, and poetically from her heart directly, to ours. She gently reminds us, in her beautifully crafted personal stories and insights, of the psychological and spiritual truth behind every human being. Each chapter invites us into the space of stillness, peace, and reflection, and ultimately a direct experience of that deeper, purer divine dimension within ourselves, the space of our true nature. So open Sarah's gift, open yourself to it, and you, like me, will be filled with gratitude and love for our one precious life and for who we truly are."

~ **Stef Cybichowski,** certified Master Transformative Coach & speaker

"You Are the Blue Sky will charm spiritual seekers with its quirky and relatable anecdotes about money, relationships, family and career, all of which invite us to explore the thought-created nature of reality and our truest essence. The simple understanding in this book grants a freedom from unnecessary suffering that is truly life-changing. I was deeply moved by the honest telling and left with a deeper appreciation for the beauty of being human."

~ **Stephanie Benedetto,** coach, storyteller and (un)marketer

"Powerful! Sarah Kostin is the friend who holds your hand and walks you down the path to joy and peace. With vibrant writing and a compassionate voice, *You Are the Blue Sky* is the perfect bedside companion, a book to be savored."

~ **Elsa Watson,** author of *Maid Marian* and *The Other Elizabeth*

you are the blue sky

Sarah Kostin

you are the
blue sky

Sarah Kostin

Understanding who you are
beyond your thinking.

You Are the Blue Sky: Understanding who you are beyond your thinking

Contact the publisher: www.soulspiredpress.com

Contact the author: www.sarahkostin.com

Editing: Chris Nelson

ISBN: 978-1-7368394-0-9

Library of Congress Control Number: 2021914014

First edition

Dedication

For our one wild and precious life

(Mary Oliver)

Table of Contents

Part One: Understanding.. 11

Burned Out by Busy 13

Floating in the Ocean 16

The Most Important Understanding You've Never Heard Of 18

From the Inside Out 22

My Missing Cat 24

Feeling Creatures 27

Part Two: Living in Story.. 33

Streaming Consciousness 35

My Baby Movie 38

Playing the Game 41

Money Fears 44

Defined by Divorce 46

Recovering People-Pleaser 48

Capacity 51

No Mistakes 56

Letting In 62

Part Three: You Are The Blue Sky.................................... 67

The Shape of Clouds 69

Returning You to You 72

Being Is not Boring 74

The Space of Love 78

One Thought Away 81

Like a Rock with Ears 84

I Am Guided 88

The Wind on a Bike 93

United we Stand 96

Connecting to the Network 99

Part Four: The Clues of Clouds..................................... 105

Turbulence 107

Moody Clouds 110

Emotional Seaweed 114

Managing the Garbage 117
Kindness of the Design 121
Relieved for a Disease 125
Fear is Working For Us.. 128
Shattering the Glass... 131
Double Parked 134
Tree Therapy.. 137
Dowsing the Well.. 139

Part Five: Of Clouds + Sky 143

Reconnecting with God 145
Spiritual Roommates 148
Infinite Doorways 151
Falling into Presence.. 154
Wisdom Spotting 156
Play Like an Otter.. 159
When We Stop Searching 161
I Walk the White Line 163
Both/And 165

Closing Poem.. 169

Did You Know? 171

Acknowledgments.. 175
About the Author 177

Part One: Understanding

If the only thing that people learned was not to be afraid of their experience, that alone would change the world.

— Sydney Banks

Burned Out by Busy

I stood on the lawn near the outdoor patio bar, watching the fading summer sunlight sparkle on the nearby river. It was Happy Hour, and live guitar music was playing in the background. I was chatting with a dear friend who was visiting our mountain town after having taught for several years in India and Europe.

I told her about my life at the time, juggling a full-time job running the children's department at my public library, teaching four or five yoga classes per week, coaching a handful of clients for almost free, practicing yoga, meditating every day and hitting the mountain bike trails as much as possible. Not to mention trying to squeeze in time with the hubby, dog, friends, and the necessary errands that compose a life.

With a gentle tilt of her head and a smirk, she asked me in that I'm-only-saying-this-because-I-love-you tone, "Do you find it ironic that you're a life coach and are the busiest person I know?"

"Hmmm" I replied. I hadn't really considered that. "That's just my normal."

"Exactly."

She was pointing, but I really didn't see. True, there was not much white space in my calendar, but my time was completely consumed with things that I enjoyed doing. It's not like I was slogging away at a corporate job in a city that I hated just so I could buy me some Louis Vuitton shoes that I would never wear. I was living the ideal mountain-style life to the fullest, seizing the day, and squeezing every last drop out of it.

That said, my wise friend was right: I was happy, but I was also exhausted.

Back then, I erroneously believed that I had to work at happiness. I thought that if I got the formula just right and had my circumstances aligned in the correct order, then I would feel happy and content. This is the way that most of us are taught. Our culture of consumerism and hustle continues to reinforce this lesson throughout our lives.

And this method does work for a while — until it doesn't.

Not long after that Happy Hour conversation, I stumbled upon an understanding of the mind that would change my life forever. It flipped everything I believed right on its head.

This understanding pointed to a spiritual truth: that our true nature is one of happiness, contentment, and peace. Because human beings are spiritual beings, our spirit can never be broken, contaminated or destroyed. It is the bit of us that is infinitely resilient and aware.

We don't have to work hard for happiness at all. We are made of it.

The reason this spiritual truth is elusive is because of one very important gift that we possess: the gift of thought. It turns out that instead of feeling the beauty of our true nature, most of the time we are feeling our thinking about our personal lives.

And let's face it, most of our thinking about ourselves feels anything but peaceful, content or ease-filled.

Rather, it's kind of like walking around wearing an itchy sweater all day and thinking that that's the way our body naturally feels. When we finally take off the sweater, our naked skin feels soft and luxurious. It is who we really are underneath.

When we finally set down our agitated thinking, we reconnect with our true self.

Floating in the Ocean

Imagine that you are floating in the ocean.

> Sidenote: I once used this metaphor with a coaching client who told me afterwards that she was terrified of the ocean. She did not find it relaxing at all. So if this is you, please replace "ocean" with "desert," "mountains," "shopping at *TJ Maxx*"—whatever helps you feel relaxed—and adjust accordingly below.

Ahem... Imagine that you are floating in the ocean.

The ocean represents your innate well-being.

Everything is flowing, you feel connected with all of life. You are both in and of the ocean. Your mind is clear and quiet. The ocean feels like home.

While you are floating, a few thoughts drift through your awareness:

This is nice.

I wish I could stay here forever.

Did I pack my beach towel?

The water feels so silky.

These are low-level thoughts; they float in and out of your awareness. You don't focus too heavily on them because you are immersed in the good feeling of the ocean. You are relaxed, calm and completely at ease.

Suddenly, a new thought comes into your awareness:

What if there are sharks in this ocean?

This thought seems more important than the other thoughts. This thought has meaning. This thought could save your life. So, somewhere in the background of your mind, your consciousness lights up this seemingly meaningful thought about sharks.

In a flash, you are no longer experiencing the feeling of floating peacefully in the ocean. You are now experiencing shark-infested water, and you feel that your life is in danger.

Your thoughts spin and grow louder in volume. You panic.

I'm all alone.

I'm not the strongest swimmer.

Did I tell anyone where I was going?

Did I turn off the stove?

How long have I been out here?

You swim to the shore, grab your flip flops, and scuttle home like a scared little crab.

Were there really sharks in the water?

Who knows?

The external circumstance does not matter. It was the *thought* of sharks that completely changed your experience. You *felt* the thought of the potential of sharks as if the sharks were really chomping at your perfectly pedicured feet.

One moment you were in a blissful feeling floating in the ocean, as if you were starring in the Disney film *Moana*. The next you were running to the shore, breathless and scared, playing the role of an extra in the movie *Jaws*.

Now how did that happen?

It was an example of the Three Principles in action.

The Most Important Understanding You've Never Heard Of

Imagine it's 1973. There is a Scottish man in his early forties who works as a welder in a pulp mill in Canada. He has a thin frame and kind eyes. He clocks in at the mill every day, does his job and goes home to his family. He's an average guy, with only a ninth-grade education. He's not particularly a spiritual seeker, but he's curious.

His name is Sydney Banks.

One day, while attending a marriage seminar with his wife, a therapist he is chatting with makes an innocent comment to him, something to the effect of, "Syd, you're not insecure — you just think you are." That simple statement sparked something inside of Syd, and he experienced what many now call his "enlightenment experience."

Through this experience, an understanding was revealed to him of how our awareness, the gift of thought, and the universal intelligence of life are all interconnected. Less than a year after his experience, Banks left his job at the mill and spent the rest of his life (he died in 2009) speaking and teaching this understanding — which he later named the Three Principles — to all who would listen.

The concept of the Three Principles has acquired many other names, such as the "Inside-Out Understanding," "Insight Principles," the "New Paradigm," or simply, "The Owner's Manual." It points to the same truth that has been told for thousands of years, just framed in a new way that feels more accessible to our modern times.

This understanding is now shared by a passionate and growing community of teachers, speakers, coaches, and counselors, and it's helping thousands of people understand where their feelings of insecurity, doubt, worry, anxiety, and sadness come from. Through realizing this understanding, more and more people are finding greater contentment, ease, and joy.

So how does it work?

In the example from the previous chapter, the ocean represents our true nature and innate well-being, a state of calm and ease. This is referred to as the principle of Universal Mind, or for the sake of brevity, Mind. It is quite different from what we typically think of as our mind, and it is not our brain.

According to Banks, Mind is the creative power and intelligence behind all life. Mind is the energy source that is operating behind the scenes for us and for all life on this planet, all of the time.

When we discover Mind within ourselves, we begin to realize the connectedness between human beings. We become aware of the flow of universal intelligence moving through us. Mind gives us the freedom and power that comes with feeling a part of something bigger than ourselves. We no longer have to strive so hard to fix, figure out or plan our life, because the universe really does have our back. Mind is the sense of inner knowing and wisdom that has helped guide us throughout our entire life.

In the previous metaphor when we were floating in the ocean

of Mind, many thoughts drifted in and out of our awareness — and we temporarily focused on one particular thought about sharks.

The principle of Universal Thought refers to the creative energy that brings words and images into our heads out of thin air. Thought is the language of Mind. Thought is the filter through which we view our external circumstances, and it gives our present moment experience its quality and texture of feeling. The external world is actually neutral, but it rarely feels that way. We are always feeling our thoughts about the outside world.

In the ocean vision, the principle of Universal Consciousness came into play. Consciousness selected the thought, *What if there are sharks in the ocean?* This attention brought that thought to life, which resulted in feeling the very "real" experience of sharks.

Consciousness is not only our awareness, but also the special effects department of our mind. Consciousness simultaneously lights up our thoughts through our attention and brings life to our thoughts via the senses. This explains why thought doesn't look like thought, but rather like an independent, freestanding reality. In other words, it describes why our thoughts appear like real life.

Before grasping what Sydney Banks is describing, it is easy to believe that our experience of life comes from forces outside of ourselves, such as life circumstances and events. Most of us operate under the assumption that our jobs stress us out, our partners make us crazy, and money — when we have a lot of it — brings us happiness. It turns out that our perception and experience of life is created via the interplay of Mind, Thought and Consciousness — from the inside out, not the other way around.

This is not a prescription for how to live life, but instead a description of how life is lived. Through the filter of us. By understanding that we are fully supported no matter what we are feeling in the moment, we are able to see through the limitations we place on ourselves through thought. We uncage our spirit and learn to navigate by joy instead of by worry or fear.

From the Inside Out

Confused? Skeptical? Don't worry, that's totally normal. In fact, if you overthink it and run this understanding through your intellect, you'll miss it entirely. Which is why most of us have not realized this simple and universal truth for most of our lives.

In a nutshell, our entire experience of life is created from the inside out. We move through life feeling our thinking about the outside world. And, it feels like real life.

When I say our entire experience, I mean everything—from our job satisfaction, to our relationships, to our views on failure and success. That old adage that money can't buy happiness? Well it's true! And neither can the perfect partner, a dream job, the flawless presentation, or the fanciest mountain bike.

Because nothing from the outside world can give us happiness.

But our *thinking* about those things can. Which is why that feeling of happiness is so fleeting.

When you feel any feeling at all, no matter how much it seems to be caused by an external circumstance, it is **always coming from you.** More specifically, it's coming from your thoughts *about* the circumstance.

The mind only works in one direction, from the inside-out.

This is counter to everything we've ever been taught. In general, we are raised and taught from an outside-in model. That our outside world creates how we feel inside. Not only are we taught that this is the way it works, it also really looks to us like our feelings are caused by circumstance. Someone says something mean to you, you feel hurt. You lose something or someone, you feel sad. You get a promotion, you feel excited.

You may think, *But wait a second! There are lots of times where my circumstance changed and the way I felt changed at the same time.* You might say for example, "I used to be worried about money all of the time. Then, I got a raise or inherited some money, and now I'm not worried about it."

That may be true, but when you look closer, you see that it wasn't the actual money that gave you more contentment. *It was the fact that you were no longer thinking worried thoughts about the money.* You had been living in the feeling of concern about money through your concerned thoughts. Then, circumstances changed and you were no longer thinking those concerned thoughts. And, voila! The feeling of concern disappeared.

You can tell this is true because someone with a lot more money than you might still be thinking worried thoughts about money. This explains why there are so many depressed and unhappy billionaires in the world. And, why there may be just as many joyful people living below the poverty line.

External circumstances are actually neutral. What we *think* about a given circumstance determines what we feel, and this looks like reality to us. Thought is the invisible middleman between circumstance and experience that shapes and molds your perception of your life.

My Missing Cat

Gryphon is a Maine Coon cat, a long-haired, tufted eared, mouse-killing, couch-cuddling, wet-food-devouring machine. Gryphon's summertime routine is to bound out of the house for his daily outdoor romp in the Enchanted Kitty Forest — the wooded hillside behind our house. If my husband or I pop home for lunch, Gryphon magically appears at home, too. He returns every evening for dinner and tuna treats, followed by lap snuggles.

One summer day, Gryphon bounded out of the house and didn't return. For two weeks, my husband and I went out every evening, shaking the canister of dried tuna treats and calling his name. We plastered flyers all over town, stalked the animal shelter, and snuck around people's yards looking in garages and sheds for our missing cat.

Then, three weeks passed and we stopped looking every night. We talked about him every evening, expressing our grief. Our conversations became more tinted with closure, with us saying things like, "He was the greatest cat", "I hope he didn't suffer" and "He lived a good life." In our way, we were saying goodbye to our best buddy of thirteen years.

Then, exactly twenty-eight days after he disappeared, I was

drinking coffee in my living room on a Sunday morning. I heard a familiar "meow" outside our glass doors. I couldn't believe it. Gryphon had returned. He was skinny and starving and purring like a motorcycle. I'm pretty sure I woke all of my neighbors with my shocked exclamations of, "Oh my f*cking God!"

During the time that Gryphon was missing, I noticed something very interesting about my thinking. My thoughts were drunk with angst and worry about whether he was suffering or if he had met some violent demise by way of a hungry fox. When I was caught up in thinking about my missing cat, I was completely heavy with grief and sadness.

At other times, when I was caught up in thinking about other things, I was perfectly happy. I only felt sad when I was in the midst of thinking sad thoughts. The formula wasn't "missing cat = sadness." I saw very clearly how the invisible piece of thought played a role: "missing cat + sad thoughts about missing cat = sadness."

This might seem very subtle at first glance. But once this idea starts to sink in, it's revolutionary. Life-changing.

We are always experiencing our thinking about a circumstance, and not the circumstance itself.

This doesn't mean I will never feel sadness again. But realizing it gives me an understanding of where my thoughts and feelings come from. And when I know that my sadness is coming from my thoughts, I actually feel freed up to feel my sadness more. I'm liberated by knowing the source of it.

It's similar to understanding the Earth's natural cycle of changing seasons. If I didn't know that winter follows autumn, I would freak out every fall when the leaves withered and fell to the ground. "All the trees are dying! It's a blight! Save yourselves!" Having an understanding of how fall operates allows me to enjoy the beauty of the dying leaves.

Similarly, knowing where our feelings come from allows us to feel them even more deeply. When we don't realize that our experience is coming from thought, then it can seem that our feelings will last for as long as the circumstance lasts.

However, all thought is temporary and transient. Therefore, all feelings pass, regardless of how intense they feel. This gives me more permission to truly feel my feelings without fear. When Gryphon was missing, I allowed myself to dwell in the sadness. I wasn't fearful that I would always be sad or that the sadness would overwhelm me. My understanding helped me to be with my experience instead of resisting it.

Of course, I was thrilled when he returned. And yes, that is just my thinking too. But I'm totally okay with that.

Feeling Creatures

Dogs live in a world of smell. Fish live in a world of water. We, humans, live in a world of thought and feeling. **We are feeling creatures.** We feel our entire experience through thought. It is truly extraordinary. No other creature feels their experience as we do. Although it may not feel like it sometimes, it is truly a gift.

You know that cultural "myth" that Eskimos have over fifty words for snow? Well it's true! Here are just a few Inuit words for snow, according to readable.com:[1]

- qanuk: 'snowflake'
- kaneq: 'frost'
- kanevvluk: 'fine snow'
- qanikcaq: 'snow on ground'
- muruaneq: 'soft deep snow'
- nutaryuk: 'fresh snow'
- pirta: 'blizzard'

---

[1] https://readable.com/blog/do-inuits-really-have-50-words-for-snow/

- qengaruk: 'snow bank'

Because the Inuit live in a world of snow, they have developed language that is nuanced to describe the variety of textures and qualities in order to navigate the landscape.

Similarly, we have hundreds, maybe thousands of words for thought. We just don't realize it because we call them feelings.

Sad, angry, jealous, vengeful, frustrated, worried, anxious, joyful, happy, elated, excited and ecstatic. We live in a world of thought / feeling. Like the Inuit, we have developed nuanced language to describe the myriad of feels to help us navigate our inner landscape.

We are mostly taught that thought and feeling are two distinct entities. Thinking involves planning, remembering, organizing, and rehearsing imaginary conversations with people we will probably never meet. (Maybe that last one is just me?)

Thinking is considered an intellectual pursuit. In school, we are graded on our thinking—right, wrong, smart, stupid. Someone who is labeled a "thinker" is considered to be analytical, calculated, a planner, and they are often seen as *un*-emotional.

It is a commonly held view that emotions are the *opposite* of thought. If thought comes from our heads, then emotions—happy, sad, horny, funny, manic, frenzied—come from our hearts.

So it is quite a shocking premise to state that **emotions *are* thoughts.** Or more accurately, emotions are the shadows of thought. When we look more closely, we see that both emotions and thoughts are energy. In fact, they are different flavors of the same energy. Sometimes that energy seems more like thinking; it takes the form of planning and strategizing. At other times, the energy feels like worry or insecurity.

When we experience the energy in the form of words and

images in our mind, we label it "thought." When we experience the energy as certain emotions, we label it "feeling." It's really all the same energy, and it's all coming from inside of us.

Emotions are thoughts with different feelings associated with them. Just as I can touch the table and notice it has the feel of a table, or touch my arm and notice it feels like an arm, I can observe that a certain thought has a feeling of sadness while another has a feeling of anxiety.

For example, I notice the external circumstance of being physically alone. I may think, "I am tired of being alone." Suddenly I begin to experience the feeling of loneliness.

It appears as though the external circumstance of being physically alone causes the emotion of loneliness. But, remember that sneaky, invisible middleman between external circumstance and felt experience? Thought! Until we realize this, we skip right over the thought and blame the external circumstance for causing the feeling.

External Circumstance + Thought about external circumstance = Emotion

Physically alone + the thought "I'm tired of being alone" = Loneliness

More often than not, there's not much space in between the external circumstance and the feeling, much less the thought and the feeling, and we miss the causality. We only feel the feeling. It's as if the equation looked like this:

Physically alone = Loneliness

But as we grow our awareness, we begin to see that we create the feeling through our thought, not by the external circumstance of being physically alone.

How else could I explain that sometimes when I am physically alone, I feel great. I have thoughts like, *I love my independence! I need my quiet time to recharge. I really am an introvert.* Then, other times, being physically alone makes me feel desperately lonely. I am plagued by low thoughts like, *Nobody loves me! Everybody hates me. I guess I'll go eat worms.*

Again, the difference is not in our circumstances but in our **thinking about our circumstances.**

Thought and emotion are not distinct from each other. Emotion is more like the residue of a thought. Kind thoughts leave a sweet residue, like honey on our lips. Insecure thoughts leave a sticky residue, like gum stuck in our hair. One thought has the quality of worry, so I feel worried. Another thought has the texture of despair, so I feel desperate. We innocently mistake the residue of our thoughts for something separate from us, something coming from outside of us, when really it's all coming from within.

Invitation to the Reader

Pick a circumstance or situation in your life, like driving to work or going to the grocery store. Pay attention to how you feel as you engage in the routine, and notice if you feel the same way about it from day to day or moment to moment. For example, if you commute to work every day, is your experience identical each time, or are there days when you're more or less stressed, preoccupied, happy, depressed?

If your experience varies, what is the variable that changes if the circumstance stays the same?

Pay attention to your thoughts, and notice how they shape your experience.

Where do your feelings come from?

Do you feel your feelings when you're not thinking about those feelings?

Try on the idea that our experience is shaped from the inside out, and not from the outside in.

Part Two: Living in Story

"We are not human beings having a spiritual experience.
We are spiritual beings having a human experience."

— Pierre Teilhard de Chardin

Streaming Consciousness

It's storytime at the Library. Snow boots are strewn across the floor, goldfish crackers crunch, and caregivers hustle in their young children. Thirty-two toddlers sit crisscross applesauce on the floor facing me, Miss Sarah the Librarian, waiting for the stories to begin.

A hand shoots up into the air. I nod at the blonde-haired girl wearing an enormous blue, plastic watch on her small wrist.

"I got a new watch! It's Ana and Elsa," she says proudly.

Another hand shoots up. "I have new boots!"

"I'm wearing camo pants!"

"I have a giraffe stuffy!"

When the room gets quiet again, I start singing our regular song, "Open Them, Close Them." Before I'm finished, a little girl, no more than two years old, wanders up to me in her pajamas and clunky snow boots. She holds up a finger with a bright green band-aid on it. She opens her mouth to speak, but I hold up my index finger to gently motion to her to wait until the song is over. She stays there as I sing to the crowd, opening and closing her mouth, desperate to tell me something. She's being so patient; her words are bursting to be told.

I finish the song and put a gentle hand on her back. "Good job waiting," I tell her. "What did you want to say?"

The room is silent, all eyes on the small girl with barely any hair and bright blue eyes. She holds up her finger and shouts, "I have a band-aid on my boo-boo!" The crowd bursts into laughter.

We chuckle when children do this, but adults are the exact same way. A thought comes into our vision and it feels like the most important thing in the whole world. *My boss is a big meanie and I hate my job and I don't get paid enough and I have that huge medical bill due next week, and that's all I can think about that's shaping my entire reality right now!*

It's like scrolling through Netflix or Hulu to pick a good show to watch. Our thoughts are like the rows of choices that flick across the screen. Our consciousness watches the shows click by, silently judging— *too boring, too scary, super cheeseball* —searching for one to focus on: *ooh wait, I love* Working Moms!

Similarly, our attention homes in on a particular show in our mind, hits "enter," and then sits back as the chosen thought or thoughts come to life on the movie screen of our mind. We become so completely engrossed in the story of our thinking that we forget not only that we are simply watching a show but that we also picked it in the first place.

As adults, we are often entertained by the intensity of children's imaginations. A young boy dresses as Batman and believes all day that he *is* Batman. A little girl adopts a stuffed animal as her very best friend and holds long, intimate conversations with it in hushed and serious tones.

It's funny how we assume that we grow out of this habit as adults. It's not true. We don't grow out of our imaginations. Our storylines just become boring, more "realistic" as we move into adulthood. We believe our storylines of how the world works— about money and business and relationships and success—just as strongly and fiercely as we believed in being Batman when we were young.

Our imaginations do not diminish as we age. They just become limited.

We are still creating and living into our made up stories as intensely as we did when we were little. It's just that our movies are not as fantastical as they once were. They are just about us.

Contrary to how it feels, our life circumstance is actually neutral. Nothing is innately bad or good, inherently stressful or depressing. There are no malicious snow storms or beautiful rainbows. There are only snowstorms and rainbows. We create a story about the event based on how we perceive that it affects us personally.

The movies in our mind are so rich, seductive, and well-produced that they sweep us away from the present moment. They sweep us away from the truth of who we really are.

My Baby Movie

For most of my life, I thought it was guaranteed that I would be a mom. I grew up in a big family, the youngest of five kids, and I have always loved being around children. I just assumed that getting pregnant and having babies was easy and inevitable. As time marched on, life showed me that it was neither. And that nothing can be assumed.

For a long time, I believed wholeheartedly in my thought-created movie entitled, Must Have Baby. I thought, *I will feel content once I have a baby. Being a mom looks so fulfilling. Babies are full of joy and poop, and so much love. I will be a great mom.*

Then, after years of not getting pregnant, my movie started becoming less hopeful and more resentful.

There is an episode of the television show *The Simpsons* in which Homer dies from eating too many donuts. He is condemned to Hell and sent to the "Lab of Ironic Punishment," where he's force-fed donuts by an automated machine for eternity.

Working in a children's library while thinking that my happiness was contingent on getting pregnant was a lot like living in the "Lab of Ironic Punishment." The children's section of the library is filled to the brim with adorable babies, perfect toddlers, and beautifully pregnant women. The one thing that weighed heavy on my mind—wanting to get pregnant—played out for me in real life on a daily basis.

"Yup, we're having another one!" I overhear a mom say to her friend. "We just keep crankin' 'em out."

"Somebody shoot me now, I'm going to have a house full of boys!"

"You're so lucky. You must have so much free time with no kids."

"Do you have kids? No? Oh, you wouldn't understand then."

Now, I know that none of these comments were made with malicious intent. These people were merely speaking from their thought-created reality in the moment. It was innocent.

I could see that my negative thinking was creating my own misery, so I strived to be more positive. *I will remain unattached. I will be happy with kids or without. If it's meant to be, it will be.*

To make myself feel better, I created a positive backup plan. I decided that I would either have children and be happy and blissful and stay home and cook meals and take them to soccer practice and fingerpaint and sing silly songs . . .

. . . or I would not have children and I would travel the world as a yoga instructor and be a free-roaming spiritual teacher, wearing long, flowy sarapes and never wearing shoes again.

To save myself from the disappointing film of *Baby Brings Happiness*, I innocently created a second movie called *Yoga Teacher Travels the World*.

Now I had two movies stuck on repeat—becoming a mom or a successful yoga teacher. That was it, the only two options that I allowed myself. I would get very frustrated, depressed, and sorrowful when neither of those two options manifested in my life. I felt unmoored by the great and powerful feeling of "not enough-ness."

I had made up only two acceptable scenarios of what my life could look like, neither of which were happening in real time. As a result, I felt terrible.

The kicker was, I had created those two imaginary storylines in the first place!

I had become so wrapped up in my thinking about having a baby that I was missing out on the life I already had, which was pretty amazing. When I looked again, I found that I already had it all: the ability to love, to connect, to laugh, to learn, to get it wrong, to get it right. I actually had access to everything I thought having a baby could bring me.

It was all here just waiting for me to climb down out of my head and notice.

Playing the Game

Seeing the story I was creating around getting pregnant did not make the story disappear. It just shifted my relationship to it. My desire for kids is still there in the background of my thoughts, but the desire differs from day to day, depending on my mood.

When I'm in a high mood, feeling confident and joyful, I see the desire to have kids as a great idea, but I'm also content if it doesn't happen for us. My high-mood vision is me on Broadway singing show tunes with a chorus of dancers behind me belting, "*C'est la vie!* Whatever will be, will be!"

In stark contrast, when I'm in a low mood—tired, exhausted, and drained of energy—I'm humming a very different, off-key tune. I see an image of me as a shriveled, miserly woman on the streets with a service dog and mismatched socks reading Tarot cards in front of the library. This stark vision creates feelings of despair, loneliness, and grief.

The desire to have kids is still there no matter my mood. However, I suffer from the desire when I attach my happiness or self-worth to the outcome. We often see *wants* as *needs*. But other than *needing* a carnitas taco when I am starving, when a want feels like a need there's probably some extra value being placed on it.

This baby will bring me fulfillment. This bike will make me a winner. This job will make me feel financially secure.

My teacher, Michael Neill, once spoke with me about my desire to have kids. At the time, I was stuck in my head about it, really wanting to know if I was going to have kids or not so that I could "move on with my life." The not knowing if I was ever going to become a mom was clawing at me.

His coaching led me to a massive insight: there were more than just the two options of having or not having kids. There was a third option. I could live my current life, continue to try to get pregnant, and be in the not-knowing if it was going to happen or not. I could embrace and live in the unknown instead of fighting it. I could stop creating a story around what it means to have or not have kids and just be "lifed" by life.

It seems so simple now, but this was an enormous shift for me. Prior to this, I had not realized how vested in and attached I was to those two scenarios. I was breathing life into two separate fantasies through my constant attention and focus on them. There was zero space for the mystery of life to deliver me a third or fourth or even a fifth option.

I could actually find contentment in the space between those two fantasies that I had created for myself. That space holds infinite possibilities. It was possible to remain unattached to the outcome and enjoy playing the game. Because I saw for the first time that I would truly be okay no matter how the game turned out.

By leaning fully into "I don't know," I gave myself permission for life to live through me. There is magic and endless possibility for surprise when I live this way. Because what is on the other side is just a new flavor of thought—elation or rejection. Both can be handled in the same way, by being fully present with whatever feeling arises.

Not knowing where life is going to take me is now one of the very best parts of the ride. How boring to know, to have it all figured out, how stale — and utterly impossible.

Happiness does not exist at the end of the rainbow. It *is* the rainbow. The rainbow right under my feet, on the path I'm currently on. We are fundamentally okay whether or not we acquire the pot of gold.

Money Fears

Growing up, I went to Catholic primary school, CCD on Sundays, participated in Lent, Ash Wednesday, no meat on Fridays, and a vow of silence on Good Friday. I would help my mom deliver the Eucharist to home-bound parishioners and to community members in the Meals on Wheels program. I prayed every night and pretty much adopted the Golden Rule of "do unto others" as my life mantra.

The beliefs I inherited around money were that if I had no money, then I was virtuous and a good person, just like Jesus. After all, he dressed in a tattered robe and wore the same sandals every day. If I had any extra money, I was to give it away to those in need. So inadvertently and subconsciously, I had created a world where if I had more than my share of money, I was a bad person.

(Sidenote: my sister once told me that she did not inherit this same belief pattern and thought I was crazy . . . Just more proof that we are creating our own realities from thought.)

I had been unknowingly operating under this premise my whole life, which formed the basis for all my decisions. Heck, it is even why I became a public librarian, one of the only professions in the world that does not deal with direct commerce. We give everything away for free!

What this looked like in numbers was that no matter how much money I made, I would always spend it down to zero or go into debt. I assumed that I was just "really bad" with money. I didn't understand why my bank account would be empty every month, even when I earned pay raises or made extra income with side jobs.

When I finally saw that I had been operating from this false premise, it blew my mind.

It makes perfect sense that a person who is living from the idea that having money is a mark of shame would unconsciously make sure that they never had any money in their bank account.

Behavior changes quickly with insight. Once I saw fresh, I paid off a credit card debt that I had thought would not be paid off for months. My savings began to grow for the first time in my life.

In the past, paying off my debt would have sent me into a spending spree. I would feel physically uncomfortable at not owing any money, at having enough. My stomach would clench, and I would get a manic, hyper feeling of energy coursing through my body that could only be resolved by spending money, putting myself back in debt.

With insight, I saw my finances afresh. The guilt and shame around money simply fell away. I didn't have to take a money management class or learn how to budget. In identifying the false story around money, it vanished. It seems laughable to me now that this movie had played for so long without me realizing it.

Defined by Divorce

"It's never too late to have a happy childhood."

— Michael Neill

I spent a lot of my adult life stuck in victimhood around my parent's divorce, which happened during my teens. In reality, I had a tremendously happy and blessed childhood. However, I fixated on the one dark spot of my youth.

For the entire decade of my twenties, I allowed this experience as "the child of divorce" to define who I was. I somehow felt that it made me more dark, complex, or interesting to have an undercurrent of sadness underlying my otherwise happy-go-lucky exterior. I wanted people to think, "Wow, she's so deep."

Just last year, my husband and I were out to dinner with another couple. They asked about my childhood. Like a robot, I dove into the old story of my parent's divorce. I might as well have placed a dead bunny on the table. The energy at the table quickly turned sour. I could actually see the story poison the good vibes that we had just been experiencing. That was my first glimpse into the fact that I was holding on tightly to this old narrative.

After dinner, I mentioned to my husband that I regretted telling that story at dinner. He responded, "Yeah, it's time to let that go. That's such an old story. I'm surprised you're still telling it."

Why hadn't he said something before!? Perhaps he had, and I just never paid attention. Insights are funny like that. Insight comes from inside ourselves. I have to see it for myself or it will never stick.

A short while later, I found my baby book at my mom's house. It was filled with photos of a smiling, laughing, running, singing, dancing, playing young girl who appeared to be absolutely in love with life. It was me.

I had somehow forgotten the pure love and bliss of my childhood. Sure, the divorce still happened. It affected me in an emotional way as a young person. But the pictures reminded me that there was so often a house full of loving, caring humans that adored me, regardless of the divorce.

Memory is old thought brought into our awareness. I was bringing up old thoughts about the divorce into my present awareness thirty-some years later and acting as though it was still happening.

Thoughts by their nature are ever-changing. The divorce memory was just a thought that I chose to cling on to for far too long. A thought that I breathed life into through my focus and attention.

When I recognized that I was living in old thought, I was able to see the truth that my childhood was actually pretty wonderful. All of that old thinking dropped away, and I was free.

Recovering People-Pleaser

"No one can make you feel inferior without your consent."

— Eleanor Roosevelt

Do you remember those Charmin paper towel commercials from the 1980s? The little girl struggles to roller skate without falling down, so she goes home and stuffs her sweatpants with paper towels to cushion her fall.

Well, we are kind of like that. Our thoughts are like paper towels, surrounding us and protecting us from how we see the world. We are not feeling the world skin to skin. There is a layer of thought in between that tells us how we feel about the outside world while we're touching it.

When I began to see the inside-out understanding, I started taking my own personal thinking much less seriously.

Then, a remarkable thing happened: I began to take *other people's* personal thinking less seriously too.

This was a game changer for me. Even though I've tried to fight it all my life, I do care what other people think of me. I try not to let it influence me, or to overly attach to it. But it's always there — that desire to be appreciated, approved of and validated. Let's face it, I am a people-pleaser—in recovery.

When I began to see that my thoughts were creating my in-the-moment experience, the walls started to come down. When someone would say something I didn't agree with, I could see, *Oh, their thoughts are appearing very real to them right now.* And I could also tell myself that their thoughts were not any more solid at that moment than my thoughts.

I have been with my husband for over sixteen years. He has always loved to tease me. It's his way of showing affection, something he never outgrew from his middle school days. Sometimes he would tease about how I always drive the car with a giant mug of hot tea in one hand, or how I love to be in control of the music, or that I'm competitive when playing ping-pong. Small things.

Well, depending on my mood, sometimes that teasing went over well and sometimes it really didn't. When I was in a good mood, I could laugh at myself along with him. If I was in a low mood, his teasing felt like judgment, which usually resulted in me becoming a puddle of tears.

One summer evening we were strolling down the sidewalk after dinner, taking in the beautiful Alpenglow as the sun set in the mountains. He teased me about something. I wish I could remember what it was. My response was totally different from what it had been in the past.

Whatever it was that he had said, I actually found it really funny. All of my defensiveness about what he thought of me just melted away. Underneath his teasing I could finally see the affection that he had for me and his odd way of showing it.

For the first time in a long time, I did not take it personally. I just looked at him and laughed and laughed. Belly-laughed.

His teasing stayed the same. It was my reaction to it that was different. I didn't get caught up in my thinking about what his teasing meant. Instead, I felt a nice, warm feeling of affection.

So instead of arguing or crying, we linked arms and strolled down the street, which was dappled pink with the lowering light of the sun.

Capacity

Sometimes we avoid actions or people or situations because we are trying to avoid a feeling.

We don't want to feel embarrassed or intrusive, so we don't put ourselves out there.

We don't want to feel the sting of failure or the pressure of success, so we don't try.

We steer clear of a certain person to avoid the irritation or frustration that tends to arise when they are around.

We don't want to shine too brightly, afraid of the feeling of being judged.

We don't have to be afraid of our feelings.

We have the capacity, the bandwidth to be with any feeling.

A feeling cannot kill you.

A feeling is energy.

We feel it and it eventually passes and eases, just like a cloudy sky gives way to a blue one.

We can ride out the storm of any feeling.

~

I am hurting now. I just found out that my eggs are not viable enough to ever get pregnant.

I got the call at 4:45pm on a Friday from my gynecologist's office. The woman on the other end of the line was very kind and polite. She was not my doctor. She delivered the results of my blood test like the waitress relates the soup of the day at the local diner.

"Your Day Three bloodwork came back. It looks like your ovarian cycle is very low."

Me: "Okay, what does that mean exactly?"

"I'm not sure."

"Okay, what are my next steps?"

"Normally, you would get an HSG test and your husband would get his sperm tested."

"Ok, so let's do that."

"Can you hold please?"

I stacked and unstacked the dishwasher. My cat meowed for more wet food.

"Yes, hello, Sarah? The doctor said that you don't have any viable eggs to become pregnant. Your only other choice would be to do in vitro with a donor egg."

"Oh."

We get news, we get a phone call, we get an email that changes things. It's such a simple occurrence, a benign bump under the skin. We can feel it. The more we focus on it, the more it can grow and swell until it feels like there is no room for anything else.

But we have the capacity to hold the sad feeling while not taking on its heft and weight.

There is a strange duality that takes place. *I am okay.* **And,** *I feel disappointed, sad, and broken.* I know that I will still live a meaningful life as a woman who loves children but does not bear any of her own. And I can grieve the loss of not having a baby with my own

DNA. I am full of love and joy and tenderness. *And,* I feel the hurt, the sadness, the disappointment of not getting what I wanted.

I have not told anyone about this yet except for my husband. I am not ashamed or embarrassed in any way. What I fear is that when I say, "I can't have children," someone will respond with saying something like this:

"Sure you can. You know there's in vitro."

"Have you thought about adoption?"

"What about fostering?"

"Hey, you never know!"

Then, I may have to consider punching them in the face, smiling beatifically and deftly changing the subject.

We do that, don't we? We glaze over the hurt or sadness of someone else and we "silver-lining" it. Subtly, unconsciously saying, let's not focus on the feeling. Let's not let that one in.

I haven't told anyone because I just want to be sad. I want to hold the sadness in my arms like I would a newborn. I want to sing it soft lullabies and be stone-drunk tired at 3:00 a.m. whispering to my sadness a fairytale of a girl trapped in a tower with nothing but her long hair to save her.

We avoid doing a thing to avoid a feeling.

Here I sit, crying as I type, writing these words that I will most likely never share with anyone. Though I know they might help someone else.

I've learned that leaning into my own experience and sharing vulnerably cuts through isolation and the illusion of separateness. I know that I am not alone in my experience. For that I am grateful.

I also see my resilience underneath my grief. I am not broken, not even close. I am a whole, complete human who happens to be experiencing the texture of disappointment, the scratchy fabric of lost hope.

It is not who I am. It is just a feeling that is currently present. A feeling, like all feelings, that I can sit with without succumbing to.

That is another thing I fear about sharing this experience with people. That I will become this sad story, as I shuffle down the sidewalks in worn-out slippers. "There goes Sarah," they will whisper to each other in hushed tones. "She quit her job as a children's librarian. She can't have kids. Such a shame — the kids all loved her so much."

I can see how easy it is to slip into a feeling of bitterness and resentment against the world when it seems to have disappointed you. It feels like the bitterness protects us against the heartbreak that comes from outside of us.

But that only works when the world operates outside-in. If I believed that not having a baby was guaranteed to make me an embittered old woman then I would cut myself off from ever feeling the love and connection that it is possible to feel with any human. Not being a mother does not mean I cannot love. It does not mean I cannot nurture and hold space for others' growth.

Sometimes, I stare at small children walking hand-in-hand with their moms, or riding on the shoulders of their dads. Just today there was a brown-eyed girl with long, brown hair wearing a tiger-striped mask. Her sneakers were adorned with glittering unicorns. She stared up at me with wide eyes that crinkled on the sides, a hidden smile beneath the mask. In that moment, the whole world shrank down into this small human being and my heart filled with love. I thought, *I hope I don't look like a stalker.* I grinned and said hello. She stared right into my eyes, kind of excited that this strange woman said hello. *She saw me,* she seemed to exclaim as she skipped up the trail to catch up with her family.

Before I understood that my experience is coming from my thinking about a situation, I used to become so jealous of the beautiful pregnant women that would waddle into the library with their families. I tried hard not to stare. I cloaked myself in the comfort of tortured thoughts that really only dragged me down into a lonely abyss of victimhood. I shut myself off from the truth.

Now I see that pregnant women, with their ballooned bellies and stretched skin, show a remarkable capacity for what can fit inside. We have a capacity to hold it all — the sadness, the hope, the fear, the worry, the grief, the love, and the compassion — all at the same time. We don't have to discard one to have the other. All of the feels can swell and blossom and be together, because our energetic capacity to hold them is as infinite as our consciousness.

No Mistakes

I was experiencing a moment of panic when I quit my beloved job of sixteen years. I emailed my mentor with an email that basically said, "Holy shit, what did I just do?"

My body clenched with anxiety, eyes wide and head spinning, as I opened his response.

"Sarah, do you realize that there are no mistakes?"

I arched one eyebrow. *Are you sure?*

My mind rattled off all of the things I would be losing: a steady paycheck, benefits, flexibility, a lovely team of coworkers, a great boss, work that made a difference in people's lives, stability and — most importantly — the known.

It felt like a very real, very gargantuan mistake.

Although I didn't yet believe it, that phrase kept repeating in my head like a mantra for the next few weeks: *Do you know that there are no mistakes?*

Deep down, I knew he was right. It had been a long time since I had ventured out from my comfortable life into the unknown. I had forgotten the untethered feeling of leaping.

Seventeen years earlier I had made a similar leap as I packed my Toyota Corolla with clothes, books, and my guitar to move nearly 2,000 miles away to a town I had never visited before and where I only knew one other person. It didn't make much practical sense, but I was twenty-three and full of trust and innocence that things would work out.

And, they did.

Less than a year after I moved, I met the man to whom I am now married, started building the house that we still live in, and began work at the library — which I found fulfilling for over sixteen years. My life was steady and consistent.

Perhaps that was one of the reasons I was ready to leave. I was craving change and growth.

Still, it was not a rash decision. It had been about five years from the time I'd first had the thought that I might want to pursue a different career to actually leaving the library. What looks like a sharp left turn to people watching from the outside is often a thousand, slow baby steps in a new direction. And for me, those steps followed a path more like a hummingbird's flight pattern — definitely not always in a straight line.

It started as an itch. I followed my curiosity, flitting from flower to flower based on what felt good to me in the moment. It was an exercise in patience, self-love, and leaning in to wisdom. It was a meandering route, fueled by heart.

First, I learned web design and built websites for yoga teachers. It just so happened that one of the teachers couldn't pay me money for my work, so we traded a yoga teacher training certification. I fell in love with teaching yoga, which I did for about four years, teaching a couple of classes a week while still working at the library.

Yoga led me to pursue mindfulness and meditation, which I taught to kids at the library and the local elementary schools. Soon, I was pursuing a coaching certification focusing on mindfulness and somatic awareness.

Upon graduation, I devoured every book on coaching I could find. Then, quite by chance, I stumbled upon a book called *The Inside-Out Revolution* by Michael Neill—and after that my life was never the same. That is where I was first introduced to the Three Principles, the understanding on which this whole book, and now my life's work, is based.

I went on to study with Michael Neill through his six-month coaching program, The Supercoach Academy, where I became a certified Transformative Coach. It was then I realized I had found my next calling. Every fiber of my being told me that this was what I wanted to do with the rest of my life, and maybe even why I was put on this planet in the first place. That is how strong a calling feels when you find it.

I discovered a passion for a new way in which to help people by having deep and meaningful conversations through my work as a life coach. I was still content at the library, but I began to notice a big difference in how I felt after I coached. My whole body lit up and I felt a renewed energy that I had not felt since first starting as a children's librarian—when I had dressed up like the Pigeon from Mo Willems' books and held a sleepover inside the library to reward the high readers in our summer reading program.

Coaching was a part-time hobby for two years before I transitioned into full-time work. I kept waiting for the "right" amount of clients and the "right" amount of money in my bank account, but it never came. I spent those two years fretting about how I was going to leave a job I loved to pursue this new dream. I had many conversations with fellow coaches, crying about how hard it was to give up my old identity to embrace uncertainty. I was desperate to know that it would all work out.

Then, a funny thing happened. After diving deeper and deeper into the Three Principles, I realized that I was making up a LOT of story about what my job meant about me. I was clinging to an old identity that I had outgrown. I was also clinging to a story about what my future would look like if I pursued my passion.

I realized I was swimming in a lot of bullshit. I had been living into this belief that my career was what could make me happy or unhappy.

Then I found it.

I found contentment that was not attached to my career or my work or my identity.

Instead, that contentment had been inside me all along. Happiness comes from the inside out, not from my circumstances or environment. I looked within, and I found it.

With this discovery I realized I could be happy at the library for the rest of my life. My enjoyment of my job was always coming from how I held it in my mind. If I went to work thinking shitty thoughts like, *I don't want to be here, I'm so over this, I'm not growing*, then I would feel the experience of those thoughts for as long as I was thinking them.

If I thought uplifting thoughts like, *This is such a wonderful job, I am so grateful to work here, I love my coworkers*, then I would experience positive feelings at work.

Whether it's positive or negative, my experience is always coming from me.

Many people hear this, and think that the solution is just to have positive thinking. The only problem with that method is that it's exhausting and impossible. Since thoughts are constantly shifting and changing, it's kind of like herding cats.

It turns out, there is a third way. Just show up and be present with whatever is happening in the moment, without making up a story about it to determine whether it's good or bad, positive or negative, a challenge or a reward.

Just show up and be.

When I started to come to work in this way, I felt great. I let go of having to decide about my career and realized that I would just know. I dropped the anxiety and the agony of trying to figure it out.

I just stayed present with every human I interacted with, with every task that I achieved. You know what? It was probably the most satisfying year of my work life.

I wasn't burnt out or busy. I wasn't depressed or suffering. I just enjoyed the work of life, the life of work. And it did not take very long of living in that state of mind before the knowing came in. Suddenly, and very decisively, I knew it was time to leave.

After five years of expectations, of trying to figure it out, of listening to internal "shoulds" and "shouldn'ts," I let go. I truly saw that I would be okay no matter what.

On the day that I told my incredibly understanding boss that I was leaving, I wasn't stressed, nervous, anxious, or sad. It came from a very neutral place, and I knew that my words were coming from wisdom. It was almost like an out-of-body experience. I watched myself from above saying the words, "I'm leaving in five months." I was shocked at how grounded, peaceful, and calm I felt.

It wasn't until hours later, that the panic and anxiety set in, when I emailed my coaching mentor. He reminded me of what I already knew: *there are no mistakes.*

The circumstances of our life are neutral, and we are only (and always) making up what the circumstance means about us — good, bad, right, wrong, failure, success.

Our feelings always have our back. If I am feeling constricted, I know it is coming from a story I've made up. Anger from a story of not making enough money. Resentment from the illusion of not being seen in my job. Anxiety from overthinking what quitting will mean for my identity.

Yet when I talked with my boss I was in a place of serene calm. I felt supported and held as I spoke my truth. It felt expansive, despite the fact that it didn't make one bit of rational sense.

This raises an interesting question: if there really are no mistakes in life, then how do we know what to do?

We choose what feels good in the moment, from a space of heartfelt, good feeling. Not from an addictive, attached, or ego-driven place, but from this space of mind that is comfortable and clear.

When we are the witness to our life, and not analyzing the shit out of it, it feels spacious. Thoughts float in and out of our awareness. We see them and are not hooked by them. That spaciousness allows for wisdom, for our own inner knowing. For me, that feeling feels like joy, a deep, pure, grounded feeling of love.

When I come from that space, it's true: there are no mistakes.

Letting In

"Your emotions are 100% of the time on your side. They are letting you know the quality of the experience that you're creating at the moment. That is a big deal!"

— Mavis Karn

I lay on the bed, limbs splayed out like a starfish. My body heaved with sobs. The loss felt like a beluga whale was sitting on top of me. Heavy. Huge. Inescapable.

And then I remembered. Right, this feeling is coming from me.

I am not feeling this intense grief because I just left my job. What I am feeling is the weight of the thought: I will miss my coworkers. The density of the thought: Will anyone love me again? The heaviness of the thought: What if this was a giant mistake?

Thought feels true. Thought feels real. Thought feels like an actual whale pressed against my chest as I stare, eyes brimming with tears, at the liquid ceiling.

We simply misinterpret what our feelings are telling us. The feeling of the whale lying on my chest is not telling me that the action I took was wrong or needs to be fixed. It is telling me the quality of my thinking in that moment. It is letting me know, in a very overt way, that I am "in" an intense amount of thinking.

The way we feel in any moment is not the whole truth of the entire scene.

If I did not know that feelings were a temporary sensation created from my thought, I never would have been able to make this career transition that I know is the right move. My intense feelings were screaming at me to stop, to turn back, to reverse my direction. "You're making a huge mistake!"

The intensity of the feeling helps me to wake up to the present moment. The moment I remember is the moment that I return back to myself. Without the intense feeling I may not have ever remembered the truth. Every emotion we have is on our side, giving us the information of what our quality of thinking happens to be.

My breathing slows. My mind slows. I feel a sense of calm returning. The whisper of wisdom underneath the panicked voices reassures me, "You're okay. Keep going."

Because we are not taught what a feeling really means, most of us resist our feelings.

However, with this new understanding of the way our mind works, we realize that it's okay to be overwhelmed with sadness, grief, or loss. It's okay to want things. It's okay to not get those things and feel sad. It's okay to be frustrated, agitated, and annoyed with our partners. It's okay to love them achingly in spite of it.

We feel it all — the rage, the hurt, the injustice, the inequality, the hate, the shame, the judgment, the sadness, the doubt, the fear — and it's all okay.

The feelings are like knocks on the door of our awareness, signals that we are butting up against our patterns of thought. Instead of closing the door, which only makes them knock louder, we can open the door and invite them in.

It is only in the story that we make up about those feelings that we suffer. If we simply feel without judgment or interpretation, we can allow for it all. Letting in these emotions opens us up to the full spectrum of human experience. Letting in lets everything in: love, connection, clarity, trust, and ease.

Resilience is our true nature. We can leave a job we love, a person we love, a place we love. When and if we feel the pain of loss, we may need some time to retreat and rest. Time to allow. Without the resistance, we naturally settle back into our innate equilibrium. We return to balance with each other, with the planet, with ourselves.

Only in letting in can we truly let go.

Invitation to the Reader

Notice the various movies that continue to play in your head.

Here are some examples of common movie titles:

- "I'm not Enough"
- "He/She is making me miserable"
- "I deserve Better/more/different"
- "I'm too tired/old/young/experienced/ inexperienced /cool/nerdy/shy/outgoingto do that"
- "I don't have the time/money/ energy"

What would it mean for you if you saw that these are merely movies that you have been running in your mind for too long?

What would you do in your life if there were no mistakes?

Part Three: You Are The Blue Sky

"You ARE this universe. And you are creating it at every moment."

— Alan Watts

The Shape of Clouds

There were two young sisters standing in a park, arguing. One girl pointed up toward the sky, squinting into the sun, and said, "See? It's a unicorn. That's its horn, and those four stripes are its legs. Right there—it's galloping through the air."

Her sister, who had long, dark braids, said, "No it's not." She pointed to the same cloud. "It's a dragon. See? There is its long tail, and there is its mouth breathing fire and all the villagers running away from it."

The girls argued back and forth, the fight nearly escalating to screams and tears, when their dad walked up. "What's going on, you two?"

"Dad!" they both whined.

"Doesn't that look like a dragon?" said the one with the braids as she pointed at the cloud.

"It's *not* a dragon!" said her sister. "It's a unicorn!"

Then, almost in unison: "Which is it? Who's right?"

Their father gazed up into the sky at the swiftly changing clouds and said matter-of-factly, "I'm afraid neither of you is right. It's just a cloud. Look!" He gestured to the sky and then walked away, leaving his two daughters in stunned silence. They stared up at the sky, which no longer held a unicorn or a dragon, just fluffy, white clouds tossed by the wind.

~

When I was young, I would lie down in the tall grass with my head resting in my hands and stare at the passing clouds for hours. I loved to watch this magical, shape-shifting spectacle in the sky. *It's a bunny! It's a bicycle! Oh, now, it's a bearded wizard eating a pterodactyl.* It only took a few moments for the wind to shift and the old shape would completely disappear, transforming and crystallizing into something new.

Thoughts are a lot like clouds. Thought is a neutral, formless energy that comes into our personal mind in the form of words or images. For a moment the thought holds a certain shape. We "see" the shape in our mind briefly and then, just like clouds, it shifts and changes into a new thought and a different shape. We call this process thinking, and we are doing it constantly.

We can have a thought about work, followed by a thought about chocolate, only to remember that it's time to meet a friend for tea. This is the natural flow of thought — transient, moving, and ever-changing energy. If we don't pay much attention to the thoughts, they will drift in and out of our awareness naturally, never keeping one shape for too long.

However, it is rare that we don't pay attention to our passing thoughts, especially when we are having thoughts about ourselves that look far more meaningful than other thoughts. *How am I going to get my kid to do her homework? What am I going to say to my boss? Why do I feel so anxious?*

The boundary of a thought is like the boundary of a cloud: blurry and ill-defined, with the soft edges of a watercolor painting. However, our focus and attention on a thought darkens the boundary lines, making them more distinct, as if they're drawn with a thick Sharpie marker.

When we define our clouds with solid lines and shapes we convert the neutral energy of thoughts into concepts, meaning and stories that appear solid. We then see the shapes of cloud-thoughts float by across our awareness.

"Oh look, this cloud of thought is my marriage."

"This one is all of the money I don't have."

"This one is the tropical vacation I can't wait to take!"

The more thinking and attention we pay to these thoughts, the darker and darker the clouds get, until they become so heavy that they can no longer flow across the sky. And they no longer look like thoughts; they look (and feel) like real life.

We start to feel the stress of overthinking, so we try to have **better thinking** about our life. But positive thinking is still thinking. It only adds more clouds to the already congested sky, making it even darker. With our attention, we form the thought into something solid called stress. We feel stress in our bodies, burrowing its way into our shoulders, neck, and back.

When the clouds become real, heavy objects in our life, we avoid, we distract, we replace, and we cope. We create a million strategies for managing the clouds.

But guess what? All this time they are still just clouds! They will move and shift and transform on their own without us. In fact, our continued attention is only helping them maintain their shape, prolonging the agony, if you will.

Most of us, myself included, have spent the majority of life managing or shaping clouds. We completely forget that the more important aspect of ourselves is not the clouds at all, but the blue sky.

Returning You to You

You have felt it. I know you have.

Perhaps it was during an activity—skiing, biking, running, yoga, paragliding, golfing, walking, painting, singing, dancing, or making love.

Maybe you felt it during times of little or no activity—meditating, drinking coffee, showering, driving, or vacuuming the living room.

Or, it was there during intense moments in your life — the birth of a child, the death of a loved one, moving to a new town, returning to a childhood home, dealing with a crisis, or when faced with a physical challenge.

It may have felt like clarity, knowing, spaciousness, contentment, joy, or love. A feeling both of emptiness and abundance at the same time.

I know you have felt it because it is always there.

It is a space.

It is the blue sky.

It is your true nature.

It is your spirit.

It is you.

What really happened was that the activity allowed you to drop out of your personal thinking for those few moments to feel it. We touch the space and then we mistakenly attribute the circumstance to the feeling. We think, *I only feel this when I am doing yoga or when I'm writing or when I'm laughing with my kids.*

Each one of those activities or circumstances is merely a doorway into an infinite space that is always here, waiting. I refer to this space as the blue sky.

The blue sky represents the spiritual side of us that never goes away. It is both expansive and infinite. The blue sky is capable of holding space for clouds but it is not consumed or identified by them. Even on an incredibly cloudy day, when the sky is dark and ominous, we know that the blue sky is still there. Even if we can't see or feel it.

The blue sky also represents the space before thought. Before thought contaminates our experience, we are whole, complete and perfect. In the space of sky is where our peace, wisdom, and well-being reside.

Our connection to our true nature is hard to feel because it gets covered up by the clouds of our personal thinking. Our true self is not missing, lost or damaged. It has only been tamed and caged by the steel trap of our intellectual mind.

The only thing that is ever in the way of your blue sky nature is one cloud. Just one thought between you and everything you seek.

The Blue Sky, Mind, God, The Divine, Mother Nature, Flow, the Field, or the Universe—by whatever name we use, language is pointing to an invisible force beyond us, of us, in us, and running through us. Whether we recognize it or not, we are all a part of the intelligent design of life.

Simply by turning our attention away from the clouds of thought and toward our blue sky nature, we return to ourselves.

Being Is not Boring

"We are either now here or nowhere."

— Baron Baptiste

Many people find it hard to quiet the mind. This is completely understandable, since our minds are made to hold thought. It's part of our design as spiritual beings who think.

The work is not necessarily to have less thinking, but to hold our thinking more lightly, to feel the sensation of getting lost in thought, sped up by thought, or hijacked by thought less often.

Our thoughts seem so compelling. But we are the ones making them compelling. Left to their own devices, thoughts are actually neutral. No more enticing than a day-old bagel left on the countertop. Sure, you could heat it up, slab some cream cheese on there, maybe some smoked salmon and a caper or two. With your attention and effort you CAN make the bagel more appealing. But it requires effort.

Similarly, thoughts are not compelling without our consent. It is simply a mental habit to dramatize our thoughts and become seduced by them. The answer to letting go of unwanted thoughts is somewhere along the lines of, well, just stop making them so appealing!

We are Thinking Beings. Our awareness can only ever be in one of two places: the ever-present now of our being, or our personal thinking. We are either now, here—or nowhere. It is like an on-off switch. We don't have to make an effort at being. Simply, when our attention is no longer in our thinking, we automatically fall into our being state.

To illustrate my point, consider if we can hold any of these two feelings simultaneously: peaceful and preoccupied, content and compulsive, restful and restless, or clear-headed and confused. They are all either/or scenarios, virtually impossible to feel at the same time. One represents a being state, the other a thinking state. Can you guess which is which?

When we are NOT caught up in thinking, our senses become hyper aware. The sounds of the blender crushing ice, the music playing overhead, the firmness of the countertop. We hear, see, feel, and touch the outside world with a renewed aliveness and reverence. *Was this tree always so crooked? Has that mailbox always been orange? When did that plant die?* We wake up to the world around us.

Our being state is only found in the now, in the space before thought. There is an expansive quality to the *now*. It is simultaneously infinite, and aware of itself. It is both creative and intelligent. It is a web of invisible energy that moves through each and every one of us. Connects us. Informs us. Forms us.

The trick is not to think too hard about it. If we *think* about being, then we are no longer *in* our being. We are in our thinking. It's so tricky!

We have to *feel* our being. To me, my being feels calm, contented, and ease-filled. It feels like there is absolutely nowhere I have to be, nothing I have to do, and that I am completely whole just as I am. Once we really see this, then we are no longer bored by being. Being becomes the most interesting, surprising, and enlightening state there is!

I will never forget one seemingly ordinary moment when I was sitting outside of a yoga studio, barefoot and drenched with sweat after practicing in a class in over 100 degree heat, packed mat to mat with other drenched, nearly-naked bodies. Next to the stoop where I sat was a flower pot filled with colorful begonias and petunias.

A bumblebee had landed on one of the purple petals. I watched the bee's tiny legs gracefully maneuver on the flower. I noticed its five eyes with awe and curiosity. Its paper-thin wings looked too fragile to lift its large, fuzzy body. I don't know if I sat there for a minute or an hour. The whole entire universe seemed to fit inside that moment. The bee, the flower and the air hummed and shimmered with a pulsating aliveness.

I was the bee and the bee was me. There was no separation.

Perhaps you have had a similar experience? A moment when time stood still and you were filled with presence. This might have seemed like an anomaly, a one-time occurrence. The truth is, this feeling is our true nature. It is our blue sky.

Peace, contentment, joy and ease. These lovely feelings are not results of actions; they are feelings from our being state.

For a moment, when my mind rested in the space before thought, I caught a glimpse of my true nature. I just had no idea that that was who I was. Who we all are.

Recognizing the blue sky within ourselves is simply a shift in our attention. So many of us have lived our whole life in the clouds of our (oftentimes) negative thinking. Our focus has made the clouds grow gray or even black, and now they obscure the blue sky.

But as we notice the being side of our nature more, patches of blue start appearing from behind the clouds. Our shift in focus naturally allows the clouds to dissipate.

At first this shift may feel like an act of trust. It can be helpful to remember that trust is a marathon. We don't expect to run a marathon off the couch with no training. We start where we are, which might mean walking around the block every day, and slowly build to further and further distances. After a certain amount of time, we are ready for the marathon. Similarly, we build trust in the blue sky by starting right where we are and paying attention to the blue sky a little more every day.

The Space of Love

I attended a breathwork workshop in a beautiful yoga studio with sliding glass doors that overlooked a briskly flowing river. The facilitator wore khaki linen pants and a crisp white tunic that contrasted his deeply tanned skin. He was the kind of handsome that comes with age — smile lines highlighting his eyes and flecks of gray peppering his dark hair.

There were about thirty people in the room, wrapped up in their snuggly blankets and fuzzy slippers, breathing together.

During the breathwork people made noise. It was distracting at first, almost comical to hear strangers making guttural, and yes, sometimes sexual-sounding moans.

I focused on the rhythm of my breath. My body felt enormously heavy, like an elephant was sitting on my legs. My glutes and hamstrings clenched against the floor. My fingers clawed up like Tyrannosaurus Rex hands and felt tingly. I forced myself to relax.

Forty-five minutes into the circular breathing, we held our breath for as long as we could, and that's when the magic happened. Historically, I am not a great breath-holder. As a kid, I panicked being dunked in a swimming pool or waiting for hiccups to go away.

Ambient music played over the speakers. An entire song played out while I was holding my breath. It felt like I could hold my breath for an eternity! Instead of panicking, I became serenely calm. I was floating in this space between being in my body and being outside of it.

Oh, I thought, *this is what it's like to die.*

I relished that feeling of being dead. My ego had dissolved and I was floating in this great in-between. I thought of my cousin, PJ, one of my favorite humans on this planet, who had passed away fifteen years ago. I smiled at the realization that this was the space in which he now dwelled.

At some point the breathwork facilitator gently placed his thumb on a space in the middle of my forehead. A vision exploded in my head—a deep, bright-purple light shaped like a diamond. I felt pulled in by the purple light as it pulsated. The diamond shape morphed and oozed into an elephant head, which then spoke to me.

It may sound like just a trippy visualization, but the message was about love. According to the holographic elephant in my head, all there is is love. My work in life is to love my husband and his family and my family. To love all of the kids and families and friends in my community. Just to love, love, love. The space underneath all of our thinking is love. I felt absorbed and cloaked in love.

I gradually eased back into a normal breathing pattern. I felt so calm and peaceful. The music changed from a fast-paced tribal beat to a soothing song about returning home. The feeling of love continued to wash over me.

We were called back into our bodies, back into the room. I woke with a huge grin on my face, the feeling of love saturating me from head to toe.

It didn't matter to me that the visions might simply be a

physiological by-product of chemicals in my brain and a lack of oxygen. It was a beautiful feeling. I touched the space of love and remembered that it is always available to me.

Love happens when we drop down from our personal thinking and truly connect with a human being—that includes ourselves—without judgment, evaluation, or expectation.

When we slow down and connect with ourselves we call it "self-love." When we are present with our partner, we call it "romantic love." When we are in the moment with our children, we call it "parental love." The phrases are all pointing to the space of connection that happens when thought is not present, but *we* very much are.

It is so easy to get caught up in the trivialities of our lives and miss the love that flows so naturally from us. The constant chatter of our own minds is the only thing blocking us from touching the space of love in any moment.

One Thought Away

"Love is universal. Marriage is personal."

— Sydney Banks

We are always one thought away from love.

Do you remember what it's like to fall in love with someone? At first you're consumed by being with this new and exciting human on a wild rollercoaster ride of novelty, fun, and connection. Then, a few weeks or months or even years later, you come to your senses and think, "WTF, what was I thinking?"

Well, the truth is, you weren't—thinking, that is.

It usually isn't until we enter into a relationship with the love of our life that the thinking begins. We start to judge, compare, analyze, and expect a lot from our partner. Instead of a heart-to-heart connection, it becomes more like a head-to-head connection. Two people are living with each other, but only ever seeing their thoughts about the other person. It is difficult to touch the space of love from a head full of thought.

It's funny that we call it "falling in love." It is certainly not "thinking in love" or "planning in love." It is a falling, a letting go of the kind of personal thought that normally limits our connection with another human being.

Falling in love is connecting with someone on a heart-to-heart level, without a lot of thinking. That's why this lit-up feeling of being with another human being feels so good. It is one of the things in life that seems to naturally take us out of our habitual thinking about ourselves. We fall into this natural and universal space of love that exists *before* thought.

I once coached a client who was struggling to find the "right" woman. He told me, "You have to kiss a lot of frogs to ever find your princess." He went on a lot of first dates and spent the majority of his time sizing up the women sitting across from him, categorizing and calculating them using different labels. *Too smart. Too old. Too boring.* He determined that 99 percent of them were frogs.

What he didn't see was that it wasn't the women who were the problem. The problem was his *hyper-analysis* of the women. It was his *thinking* about the women that prevented him from truly connecting. He struggled to see through his judgment to the truth of who was sitting right in front of him. He was innocently creating a wall of thought that blocked him from feeling the innate connection that can easily arise between any two people.

Love is universal to every human, even if it doesn't always seem like it. And in a world where it is almost impossible to tell who is telling the truth, love can become our guidepost.

If an idea, action or words come to you with the flavor of love, compassion, or kindness for another human being, then that is usually a good indicator that it is coming from wisdom. That it is True. Love is usually a sign that you're headed in the right direction.

If the thought has a flavor of judgment, anger or fear, that is often a sign that our thinking is not as trustworthy. I'm not saying those feelings aren't real. They feel incredibly real. It's just that those feelings are signs that the thinking is coming from the personal, and not the universal.

When we make things personal — about us — we tend to suffer. When we fall back into the universal feeling of love, we feel connected to the universal whole. Think of great teachers like Gandhi, the Buddha, Jesus — they led with love. Their power stemmed from their being. They lived as embodiments of love and compassion.

Contrary to how it appears, love is who we are. It is our birthright. And I believe that it is only when we come from a place of love that we will knit ourselves back together and begin to heal.

Like a Rock with Ears

The lone trill of a songbird, the sustained hum of a locust, the crackling of a dead branch as it knocks against a tree . . . When I listen to nature, my heart cracks open. With pure curiosity about the outdoor sounds, I am filled with a feeling of awe and wonder. *How did this planet come to be? Who made this tree? How am I here?*

Listening seems like such a simple and automatic task, like breathing. However, most people are terrible listeners. When we engage in a conversation, we are most likely listening to our own private *thoughts* about what the other person is saying instead of actually listening to what the other person is saying.

We run everything past a little listening judge that measures what is being said for accuracy, relevance, and truth. Often we are more concerned about what witty, intelligent, and remarkable words we are going to say next. Or, we are completely distracted by some irrelevant storyline playing in our heads. We completely miss the opportunity to hear.

Our thinking is silently loud.

It is possible to listen to other people and ourselves in the same open way that we listen when we are in nature. There is a magical energy exchange that happens between two people who are undistracted by their own personal thinking, with very little chatter getting in the way. We experience true connection.

During my coaching certification training, we did a listening exercise where we were instructed to partner up and share about an exciting moment in our lives. During the first round, we were told to listen to whatever our partners said with the intention of affirming or being in agreement with them.

As I listened to my partner in this way, I nodded feverishly. I grinned until my cheeks hurt. I leaned in dramatically. I quickly realized that listening to affirm the speaker was my default way of listening to other people. Perhaps fueled by my people-pleasing programming, I took responsibility for making the speaker feel reassured, understood and seen.

This isn't a bad way to listen. However, I noticed that my mind was filled with my own thinking when I listened this way. *Should I say something? Is it my turn? Am I nodding enough? How's my posture?* I was focused on me, and not really listening to my partner at all.

Then we were instructed to listen to negate, to let our partner know through our body language that we thought they were stupid, wrong, or incorrect. Listening "to negate" felt like somebody had poured a thousand spiders down my shirt. It was an awful feeling. However, I experienced a profound insight during that part of the exercise.

It was this: although I tend to listen to everyone else to affirm, when I listen to **my own inner wisdom,** *I often listen to negate.* I question, doubt, and judge myself instead of listening in an open way. Because I don't trust myself, I ignore my inner wisdom.

Wisdom whispers, but we immediately label it silly or worthless or dumb. When we are listening distracted, we miss the magic.

For the final part of the exercise we were instructed to just listen to our partner as if we were a rock with ears.

Listening with not much on my mind allowed space for wisdom to come through me. I didn't know what I was going to say until I said it. Surprisingly, whatever came through me seemed to be the exact thing needed in the moment, even if it was not the prettiest or most obvious thing to say.

When I am coaching a client in a session, I often have an image, quote, or random story pop into my mind from out of the blue. When I first started coaching, I was hesitant to share these little "hits" coming from beyond me. I have since learned that these messages are often delivered in that particular moment for just the person I'm speaking with.

I will offer it up to the client like this: "I don't know why, but an image just came to mind of a tree stump with hundreds of rings around it."

And they will say, "Yeah, that's exactly how I see it!"

That didn't come from me, just through me, through Mind. We all have this ability to connect to wisdom, if we know it is there.

As a coach I have had to learn to be an empty vessel and listen with an empty mind.

At first, this was challenging. I noticed how much thinking I had about "being a good coach" or "what I was going to say next" or trying to help. It was startling how much I missed what a client said on account of me trying so hard.

Something shifted for me when I began to listen more deeply, just like I do in nature. With curiosity, openness and love. When we do this with each other we connect in a more meaningful and heart-to-heart way. Through that connection, the client's mind slows down. And BOOM, that's when they hear it—their own wisdom! Not mine.

Whether we are in nature, in conversation, or by ourselves,

when we are a witness to the experience instead of thinking about or judging it, we are more open.

The clouds of our thinking dissipate and we return to the blue sky.

By listening in a more open way, we create space for new thoughts. We allow habitual patterns of thinking to rest, and begin to see fresh. We make room for intuition, creativity, and wisdom to come through. It may take practice, but it is such a fun practice! I am constantly surprised at the synchronicities and good luck that occur when I simply get out of my own way.

I Am Guided

I felt like I was driving my car through the blank white page of an artist's sketchbook. It was just past dawn on a Friday in December. The roads between the mountain town where I live and the Denver International Airport were covered with ice, and my tires were barely connecting with the asphalt beneath the snow. The hills and road and even the sky — heavy with stormclouds — were simply one big rolling blanket of gray and white.

It was nearly impossible to see where the road ended and began. The rumble strips along the edge constantly reminded me when I veered off course. My windshield was fogged, my wipers were covered in frozen ice, and I had about a three-inch patch of visibility through the glass.

A snowplow barreled toward me in the other lane and I realized, almost too late, that I had drifted into his lane. I swerved sharply to the right to avoid the truck. My passenger-side tires caught on the fresh snow, which pulled my vehicle swiftly off the road, just before a bridge.

I avoided an accident. But my heart raced, adrenaline pounded, and my whole body shook as tears rolled down my cheeks. I called my husband, apparently needing a witness to my hyperventilating panic attack. I wanted to turn around, but we both agreed that I was better off just pushing ahead at this midpoint in the journey.

I hung up the phone, and quite unexpectedly two lines of thought popped into my mind: *Just make it to Silverthorne* (which was the nearest town) and *I am guided.* I especially didn't know where that second thought came from, but it gave me comfort. For the next hour, I repeated my new mantra—"Just make it to Silverthorne. I am guided." —over and over again.

I made it to Silverthorne, which was etch-a-sketched in a million shades of grey. I pulled my Subaru into a *Grease Monkey* shop to see if I could get my frozen and useless windshield wipers replaced. I pulled my car into the loving embrace of a tall, cement garage as the attendant, Jesus (his real name!), kindly de-iced my windshield. Unfortunately, the *Grease Monkey* didn't have the right sized wipers. As luck would have it, there was a Subaru dealer right next door!

I sludged through the ice and snow, hoping the dealership carried the correct wipers. They did not. However, the kind man behind the counter suggested that I call one of the airport shuttles for a ride instead of living the nightmare of trying to drive myself. *What a fantastic idea!* He gave me the number of the shuttle company he used to work for. I waited on hold for what felt like an eternity. When I finally got through it was only to be told that there were no shuttles available. They were completely booked.

At this point, I was reminded of an old Chinese folktale about a poor farmer and his wise neighbor. Every time a significant event happens to the farmer he runs to the wise man to share the news. The farmer's horse runs away and he laments to his neighbor, "This is the worst thing ever!" The wise neighbor responds calmly, "Maybe so."

When the farmer searches for his lost horse, he finds a herd of wild mares. He exclaims, "This is terrific!" The wise man says, "Maybe so."

While training one of the wild mares, the farmer breaks his leg from a fall. He declares, "This is the worst day ever!" The wise man says, "Maybe so."

War comes to their country and the farmer is dismissed from serving in the military because of his broken leg. "What luck!" he exclaims to the wise man.

And so on and so on…

The moral of the story is that we never really know what is good or bad for us. It only appears that we do. Or, more accurately, nothing is inherently good or bad until we form an opinion about it. The more we can experience life without judgment, the more we open to the space of possibility and wonder.

Slightly disappointed from my failed wiper acquisition, I drove toward the interstate to proceed to the airport. The entrance ramp was blocked by police vehicles and flashing lights. The highway had been closed.

This is terrible! I thought.

Maybe so.

I pulled over on to the side of the road to check my phone for an alternate route to the airport. A few minutes later, I looked up from my screen to see a police officer sprinting down the middle of the road waving his arms frantically in my direction. I looked behind me to see the asshole he was yelling at, but no one was there.

It was me! He was furiously, nonverbally scolding me for pulling over on the side of the road.

I rolled down my window to hear him screaming, "Get off the road! Do not pull over!"

At this point, I was ugly-crying huge tears of stress, worry, and anxiety. I went to the gas station to fill up my tank and perhaps console myself with a gluten-free donut. And guess who was parked outside of the Dunkin Donuts waiting for the highway to reopen? My airport shuttle van!

This is amazing! Maybe so.

It was the exact company I had called with no success earlier. The driver had the engine running, fogging the windows and creating a swirl of warmth that wafted from the van. I timidly knocked on the driver's window and asked, "Is there any chance you're going to the airport and have a space for me in this van?"

"You bet!"

Tears streamed down my cheeks. I phoned the shuttle and booked it properly. The last minor detail left to sort was where to leave my Subaru for the week. The manager at the Dunkin Donuts, the gas station, and the nearby Wendy's all offered an unapologetic, "No way."

This is terrible! Maybe so.

The highway reopened, the shuttle driver was ready to leave. In a last ditch effort I found a different manager at the gas station. She had bleach-blonde hair, sharp eyes that were deeply eye-linered, and a thick, eastern European accent. She appeared unfuckwithable. I pleaded with her to let me keep my car in the parking lot. I gave her my phone number, endless promises, and a warm smile. She finally relented.

Best news ever! Maybe so.

I made it to the airport on time and flew without incident to Pennsylvania, where I spent a lovely, snowless week with my family. On the day that I returned, I was crossing my fingers that my car would still be parked at the gas station. I had gotten a phone message earlier that day that said if I wasn't there by noon it would be towed. I arrived at 8pm that night. My car was there, buried under a couple of feet of snow. It was there.

I tell this story to illustrate our real-time responsive intelligence, that of Universal Mind, which is always guiding us. We spend so much time living in worry or fear about the future. When difficult situations arise, they are usually not anything we could have predicted. We end up navigating them pretty well using our built-in common sense.

What is the moral of the story?

We can stop worrying so much about the future. I am guided. And so are you.

The Wind on a Bike

*"Why are you unhappy? Because 99.9% of everything you think,
and of everything you do, is for yourself — and there isn't one."*

— Wei Wu Wei

Working with kids and families at the library made it easy to
witness the pure, energetic spark of life in babies and toddlers — the
unconditioned true self that has yet to learn the rules.

Little balls of energy running on tiptoes through life, fascinated
about the tiniest thing or happenstance: the Yellow Tang in the
saltwater fish tank, the refraction of light that creates a rainbow on
the carpet, a shiny new book that happens to be written in another
language. Their hot tempers and ability to sob uncontrollably in an
instant. Their resilience and ability to bounce right back. Their
willingness to hug and fall in love at any moment.

It was also easy to see how fast they get conditioned — to snacks,
to a stamp at the end of storytime, to the touchscreen computers.
And to the constant pattering of rules from adults: "Don't stand
during storytime, don't scream in the library, not too loud, don't
bang on the fish tank glass, share your toys, take turns, hands are

not for hitting, walking feet, let's not rip the pages, say 'thank you,' be kind, one more minute."

We are born unconditioned, untarnished. We are born connected UP to something greater than us, and connected OUT to every other living thing on the planet. The language changes, but the feeling is there, that sense of the universal intelligence that is quietly, invisibly running the show. It runs through each of us; it does not change as we get older. It simply gets covered up.

From a very early age, we learn to cover it with our costume: our personality, our likes and dislikes, judgments of appropriate and inappropriate, right and wrong. We wear a mask of thinking over the bright, shiny light of our true nature.

Self-individuation is a hallmark of our childhood. It is part of our human development. We learn who we are. Then we get ourselves all entangled in that story. And then we have to unlearn. Unravel. Unwind. Un-self.

I once worked with an avid cyclist who had spent her whole life believing that her negative thinking about her body was true. She spent much of her life trying to manage these thoughts by trying to have a more positive body image, micro-managing her diet, and learning all she could about nutrition and healthy living.

During one session, as I listened to her struggling again with the same thoughts she'd been struggling with for the past fifty years, it occurred to me to ask her something: "Who would you be if you didn't have a body?"

She paused in mid-sentence, a little shocked by the question. "Wow," she said. "I've never considered that. Let me see." She got really quiet, closed her eyes, and listened. I saw a smile creep onto her lips and she sat up taller in her chair. "I can feel it. I can feel *her*. It's like this energy in the center of me." She sat in the feeling a little longer, then said, "Oh, I know. I am the wind on a bike."

She opened her eyes and we both grinned. We knew that it was true. She had found her truest self, this energy that is behind everything. It is before thought, before a name, and before a body. The language may be different for you, but the feeling is universal.

Who are you *before* your story?

When you see this, you see yourself.

Bear in mind that our true nature can feel uncomfortable to us at first since we are so used to feeling our drama. But it's not about getting rid of the drama. The story never goes away. It just stops dominating the narrative of our life. The story recedes from center stage into the backdrop of all our other thoughts about our life. In its place, the energy that takes center stage is the true you, the truest "I AM."

The true "I am" of any story is "I am the one who sees." I am pure awareness, only ever bearing witness to this life that is living through me. If I'm only ever a witness, I can detach from the outcome. I can laugh at my mistakes and cry at my losses. I can feel fully and completely whatever feeling comes through, because I am an empathetic and compassionate witness to my own life unfolding.

I am the wind on a bike, the energy beyond my thoughts, beyond my story, beyond my body, and beyond any idea of me.

United we Stand

I round the corner of the trail on my bike, skid to a stop and take out my ear buds. The music fades and I am stunned by the sound. It is like silence, but not quite. The leaves on the Aspen trees rustle in the gentle breeze, a chorus of infinite whispers falling over the forest. The melody of a lone chickadee weaves into the song, which is punctuated by the rustle of a chipmunk in the scrub oak.

My entire body exhales.

The trunks of the Aspen trees are the color of ash or smoke, with dark oval knots called "eyes." This last feature bestows the trees with the quality of apparent wisdom and omniscience. The aspen eyes are watching. Their leaves are uniquely positioned at the very tip of a stem so that when the soft breeze moves them, they appear to quake or dance. They are commonly called "quaking" or "trembling" Aspens.

Another unique feature of this Rocky Mountain tree is that they grow in stands. The species often propagates through its roots to form large groves originating from a shared root system. On the surface, the trees stand apart as seemingly individual trees, but underneath the soil their roots are linked and intertwined with the roots of the neighboring family members of the shared unit. [2]

This balance between appearing as an individual tree above the surface and the reality of being connected to a larger organism below the surface reminds me of another species I know.

Humans.

To the observer, it appears that we are 7.4 billion individual bodies walking, driving, dancing, running, riding, and flying over the surface of the planet. It is not as evident that there is an invisible force that tethers us all together underneath the surface. In the energetic plane of existence, the one that we cannot see, our roots are interwoven and entwined.

How do we know this is true if we cannot see it? We feel it. We feel its pull through feelings of empathy, compassion, and love. We feel it as resistance to our connectedness when we feel guilt, shame, anger, and rage.

Empathy is the word we use for our ability to feel another person's pain or happiness. When a friend tells us of a sad event in their lives, we cry for them as if we suffered the loss as well. It's hard — impossible for some of us — to watch a video clip of someone getting their eye poked with a needle, because it feels like we too are being poked in the eye. (Perhaps that sentence was even hard to read; it was hard to write!)

Conversely, we feel elated when our sports team wins the championship, as if we ourselves poured the sweat and worked our muscles to achieve the win. It can brighten our whole day to hear about someone else's good fortune. Strangers help strangers during accidents. They'll intervene if they see a crime occurring. They'll help out during traumatic events — like in the aftermath of

---

[2] {https://en.wikipedia.org/wiki/Populus_tremuloides\}

hurricanes or other natural disasters. In short, humans often commit acts of kindness and courage in desperate times.

Empathy isn't just evidence of our connection beneath the surface of life; it's a reminder of our true nature. Just like resilience, wisdom, and compassion, it is only ever covered up by our analytical or judgmental thinking about a situation. Consider the times when you lack sympathy or empathy for others. It's usually because we're judging their circumstance.

Well, he never should have started dating her in the first place. Serves her right for getting wasted. What an idiot!

Underneath our thinking and behavior, there is an energetic root system that is shared between all human beings and all living creatures. This energy is always pure, always true, and uncontaminated. "Misbehavior" occurs in response to the adulterated and contaminated thinking that sits on top of this shared energy. When we look beyond thinking, beyond behavior, it is possible to see the innate goodness in all of us. We are all connected.

Every single human has within them a spiritual nature. Every human has access to the blue sky part of themselves. If by some miracle, we were all to shut down our personal thinking for even one second, we would feel this connection. We would all be living in sky.

Connecting to the Network

"We are all connected to each other biologically, to the earth chemically and to the rest of the universe atomically... We are in the universe and the universe is in us."

— Neil deGrasse Tyson

Years ago, I was sitting in the passenger seat of our pickup truck while my husband drove. He was telling me that he had bought me a present. I can't remember why; perhaps it was for our anniversary or my birthday, or just because he was being kind.

I played coy. "Oooh, what is it? Okay, let me guess!"

He smiled.

"A necklace."

"Nope."

"Roller skates!"

"No."

"A snow mobile!"

"Nah."

I then did what one does when approaching an endless loop of guessing; I grabbed for the silliest thing that came to mind in that moment. I said,

"A peregrine falcon!"

Silence. I looked over at him to see the cute little smirk he gets when he has a secret.

The next day, he gave me the present in a small gift box. I opened the box and inside was a pair of earrings that he had bought from a booth at the local art fair. They were modeled after the exact feathers of a bird of prey — a peregrine falcon.

They were peregrine falcon earrings.

Another small example before I get to my point...

Last year I was visiting Sedona, Arizona, over my birthday week. I thought, "Wouldn't it be fun to get my Tarot cards read?" I didn't do any research, but I did ask the universe to please give me a sign.

The day before my birthday, I had a few moments of free time and remembered that I was going to look for the opportunity to get a reading if it presented itself. I went into the first Crystal shop I saw and asked if they did readings there. The woman who greeted me said, "Yes, we do. The woman who does it just stepped out for lunch. Can you wait ten minutes?"

"Sure," I said.

The woman returned, and the clerk introduced her to me. "This is Summerskye. She can do your reading for you."

I said, "Great, I'm not really sure what I want. But it's my birthday tomorrow and . . ."

Summerskye interrupted, "Well, it's my birthday tomorrow, too! Let's definitely do this!"

I realize that neither of these examples are mind-blowing. I simply wanted to highlight how common these synchronicities are. You probably have your own examples of this kind of thing.

My point is that while I don't claim to know how it all works, I just know that it works. There seems to be an intelligence to life that we somehow have access to, and through which we can connect to the intuition, wisdom, and clarity that are beyond our intellect.

In the context of this book, we've been exploring a metaphor of the blue sky being like Mind or universal intelligence and the clouds that drift across it our thoughts.

As I was writing this book, a friend and I fell into a conversation in which we wondered if this was how it all worked. A thought comes in from Mind and it takes the shape of a cloud in somebody's individual mind. They focus on the cloud and the cloud shifts, changes shape, then leaves their mind and heads back to the universal... only to float into someone else's mind who sees it in a slightly different way.

Maybe it works like a gigantic game of Telephone--one person whispering in someone's ear a sentence that slowly gets transformed through the filter of each individual until it comes out as completely new.

In the book *Big Magic*, Elizabeth Gilbert shares how she and another writer were both innocently and simultaneously working on a book with almost the exact same plot line without ever having exchanged a word about it to each other.

Maybe psychics and tarot cards and crystal readings are all somehow true. There is an invisible network of energy that is connected and beyond our five senses. It is intelligent. It is conscious. It is infinitely aware. What if it's like the Internet?

The Internet might be an apt reflection of something much bigger, a "cosmic" network of which we are a part. Tiny bits of data and information flow through this network--including us, as part of it--and when our heads are filled with less thought, we're more aware of that connection than at other times. Or sometimes things just "click" and two seemingly disparate bits of information—like a "random" comment from me and peregrine falcon earrings — come together and remind us that we are all connected as part of the invisible network of the universe.

Perhaps we're somehow connected through our breath. I have always felt that breath is somehow linked to our consciousness. That would explain why when I pause to breathe deeply I suddenly become intensely aware and infinitely more calm.

It doesn't matter what it is, but when I believe in something bigger than myself, life goes better. To paraphrase Alan Watts, "I am not little old me alone and afraid in a world it never made." I'm connected to everything. There is no separateness. And when I stop using my ego to create separateness, I fall into the fabric of the cosmos. I fall into everything. I fall into love.

Invitation to Reader

Do you notice that certain situations or thoughts seem to clutter your sky with clouds more than others?

Can you think of times when you were in the blue sky?

How much time do you spend in the clouds of thought?

What does being present require of you?

What is possible for you if you hold your experience more lightly?

Notice when you are now here. Notice when you are nowhere.

Part Four: The Clues of Clouds

"There is nothing more important to true growth than realizing that you are not the voice of the mind — you are the one who hears it."

— Michael A. Singer

Turbulence

I searched for the airplane's barfbag in the compartment above me, certain that my complexion was a putrid green. The elderly woman sitting next to me in the small aircraft flying over the Rocky Mountains kept inching her body further and further away from me toward the aisle.

The captain came on the speaker and said, "We're just flying through some low-hanging clouds as we descend. Nothing to worry about."

I closed my eyes and took deep, slow breaths, willing the nausea to leave. I clutched my book in my lap with a deathgrip that seemed to repress my body's need to vomit.

We descended below the clouds and the air smoothed. We landed safely, and I am happy to report that I did not need the barfbag.

Turbulence is uncomfortable. It's upsetting.

It's also temporary.

When we're in the middle of a jumble of thinking, it feels a lot like turbulence. Now, the captain of a plane knows she can't dismantle a cloud, but she can create a smoother ride by flying above or below the cloud. The cloud is just a natural part of flying an airplane through a sky full of clouds. The cloud helps the captain know where she is in the sky.

Although it may not always feel like it, we are able to navigate up, down, or through the clouds of our experience. By means of consciousness, we have freedom of mind.

Although we cannot control our thoughts, we always have a choice around where we place our attention. We get to assert our free will through our ability to shift our awareness. Whatever we are paying attention to is what we will experience. If we are not enjoying our current experience, we get to rise above the clouds simply by giving them less attention.

While flying through a cloud of thought, my experience feels choppy, edgy and agitated. The turbulence lets me know where my level of consciousness is at any given moment. *Oh, I'm just in a cloud. And, I'm not in the clear blue sky.*

I can't fix, remove or change the cloud. The cloud is a cloud. It's not personal. This cloud doesn't mean anything about me. This is just the feeling of this particular cloud of thought on this particular day. Simply by my noticing, I can rise above it.

The clouds are clues as to where our attention is being held, and I have come to appreciate the many clues of clouds:

- A sense of urgency
- A sense of life or death
- Any sentence with the word "should" in it
- F.O.M.O (Fear of Missing Out)
- Futuring
- Endless online searching of camper vans or travel destinations
- Doom-scrolling on social media
- Comparison and jealousy

- Not enough-ness
- Endless spinning thoughts
- Pressure and stress
- Burnout, fatigue and exhaustion

These are often the low mood feelings I experience while I'm in a cloud of my thinking. We hear this reflected in our everyday language: "I was down in the dumps yesterday," or, "I'm feeling really low today." We feel low, and often our impulse is to investigate why, or to do something to change the feeling. However, this only leaves us stuck in the cloud.

If we elevate above the cloud, we experience higher mood feelings, such as love, compassion, humor, and empathy. We use language to describe these states as well. "You really lifted me up," or, "I felt uplifted." The absolute beauty is that we can rise above the cloud in an instant. Simply by recognizing that we are in a cloud, we return to the ever-present now of the blue sky.

Our emotional well-being is not dependent on anything external. It is always coming from us. Noticing whether our awareness is in a cloud of thought or in our blue-sky nature automatically improves our turbulence.

We rise out of the cloud, sometimes quickly and sometimes not, to have greater visibility and a smoother flight. The bumpy cloud of our low-mood thinking is still there, far below us. But now we can see the ocean and the verdant valley below, as well as the infinite expanse of sky. We see, feel, and hear more possibility.

Moody Clouds

"The life of a thought is only as long as you think it."

— Mara Gleason Olson

I used to be a big scaredy-cat. Scared of success, scared of failure. Scared of making money, scared of going broke. Scared of hurting other people's feelings, scared they'd hurt mine. Scared to leave, scared to stay.

And I was terrified of my own moods, a victim of the lunchroom bullies of my grumpiness, irritation, and sadness. I never knew when they were coming. I was certainly unable to control them, and I definitely didn't understand why they were there.

I sobbed during commercials, when listening to a stranger tell me her sad story on the street corner, or whenever I held a newborn baby. If I had to talk about my feelings, especially in relationships, I would turn into a blubbery mess and exit stage left in a hurry. I have distinct memories of bawling in restaurants, in public restrooms, and even at my surprise sixteenth birthday party.

Sensitive, empathic, intuitive, a Pisces—I have strongly

identified with all of these labels, and I have always felt things deeply. Like many other feelers out there, I considered my sensitivity both a gift and a curse. A gift because it gave me the ability to emotionally connect with others. A curse because I often felt like a victim to my emotions, feeling out of control and overwhelmed.

I hated my moods. I coped with them with excessive exercise. I would run fifteen miles, do two yoga classes in a row, hike up a big mountain, or drink several glasses of wine. It really looked to me like my moods came from outside of me and swept me up in their careless rage. I avoided any situation that might cause a mood.

Now I know that moods don't come from outside me. They don't stalk me. They're not lurking in a darkened alley, waiting to jump me when I least suspect them. *Watch out behind that tree! There might be a bad mood hiding there!*

Instead, what I know now is that my moods are always coming from me, from the inside-out. (This isn't an invitation for self-blame; although I am the source of my mood, I am not creating my mood on purpose.)

If feelings are thoughts, then a mood is a jumbled cloud of many indistinguishable, and often unconscious, thoughts. A mood is much like the accumulation of a hundred dark clouds that creates the effect of an overcast day. Our mind has become so thick with thoughts that the sunlight cannot pierce through them, and our outlook appears gray.

When we're in a cloud of moody thinking the whole world appears dark and overcast. Contrary to what many believe and what we're often told, the low mood came first, not the other way around. It's so sneaky. The low mood causes us to see our circumstances in a negative light, so we seek to fix our moods by changing our outer circumstances.

How many times have I woken up a little irritable for no good reason? I feel my mood first, then I try to figure out why I'm so grumpy. I usually don't have to look very far to come up with a person or situation to blame for my low mood. *I must be agitated because of what happened yesterday or what so-and-so said.* And so on.

I have actually watched my intellect try to outside-in the problem before remembering that this is not how our experience works. An outside circumstance cannot create my inside feeling. It is always inside-out.

One of the reasons this is so hard to remember is that often when we change our outer circumstance, our mood lightens. But it's not because the outer circumstance changed. It's because our thinking changed!

By "fixing the problem" our mind became focused on a different task, and less focused on the moody cloud of thought. Any time our attention moves away from thought, the clouds of thought get a little thinner, and the uncomfortable mood naturally decreases. Moods disappear on their own. Just like the weather, there is nothing to fix. We only have to wait out the storm.

Being in a low mood is not a sign that something is wrong with my life. A low mood is simply a sign that my mind has sped up into a tangle of thinking. That's it. Full stop.

When I'm in a low mood, the world feels tight, constricted, and cloudy. I have lost sight of the blue sky behind the cloud cover, and my options and possibilities look limited and scarce. Being in a low mood is not a sign to think more about it. Thinking more will simply make the clouds even darker. We don't have to spend our energy fixing our feelings if we see them as a natural flow of energy coming from us.

As soon as I relax and am comfortable with my negative mood, it seems to fade. The less attention I give it through trying to fix it, the more likely it is that the clouds will naturally part and dissolve. This does not mean that I never feel moods. I am just as moody as ever, but now my moods don't last as long, and they don't overwhelm me as they once did. Moods have lost their meaning, and therefore their grip on me.

If I slow down the speed of my mind, the clouds naturally part to reveal the infinite expanse of blue sky that is ever-present behind them.

Emotional Seaweed

While on vacation in Mexico, I stayed at a place famous for its pristine, white sandy beaches. At that time there was a record amount of sargassum, a type of seaweed, prevalent in Mexico and the Caribbean. As a result, the once pristine beach had a large, dark stripe of seaweed slashed across its shore.

Many of the hotels hired workers to remove the seaweed. It looked like backbreaking, thankless work. From sunup to sundown the workers pitchforked or raked the seaweed into wheelbarrows. Then they wheeled the seaweed out to the road and loaded it onto trucks that carried it away.

For about twelve hours a day, the workers tirelessly struggled to remove the seaweed. At night, we would all go to sleep, but when we woke up the dark swath of seaweed had returned.

We watched this same scene play out day after day, and the hours of hard labor seemed like wasted effort. It reminded me of the story of Sisyphus, the mythological Greek king condemned for eternity to repeatedly push a boulder up a hill, only to have it roll back down just before he reached the top. I thought, *Perhaps the hotels could let go of the expectation that this beach needs to be pristine? What if we could all view the seaweed as a natural part of the rhythm of the Earth? Could we change our relationship to the seaweed?*

In many ways, we treat our negative emotions just like this seaweed on the white sandy beach. Everyone's seaweed is different. It might be feelings of loneliness or sadness, guilt or shame, fear or anxiety, agitation or anger. The seaweed represents any emotion that we want to remove, hide or run away from. We see this unwanted emotion as a scar blemishing an otherwise happy life. Some of us do it consciously; others of us have no idea that the seaweed is even there.

Whether consciously or unconsciously, we often busy ourselves trying to get rid of or hide from our inner seaweed. Some of the highest achievers I know are often very sad and lonely deep down. From celebrities to soccer moms, we have become very good at being busy.

Sometimes busy is just busy. But at other times the busyness is a distraction in order to mask an unwanted emotion. In those cases, we are just like the exhausted workers pitchforking the seaweed into wheelbarrows day after day.

If we shift our perception, and let go of the expectation that we need to be happy and joyful all the time, we begin to see that the so-called "negative emotion" is just a natural part of life. It is merely one flavor of energy. We are human beings after all, blessed with a full spectrum of human emotions.

It becomes a practice of allowing. We start by noticing the seaweed—the sadness or loneliness or shame—and we welcome it in. Then, instead of judging or solving, we just sit and be with the feeling. There's no need to fix the feeling because we know it is a shadow of our thinking. Since thought is ever transient and ever changing, just like the tides of the ocean, it will wash itself clean all on its own.

We could use all of the time and energy that we would have

spent shoveling out the seaweed to do something else, like stroll aimlessly, barefoot, along the messy shore.

Managing the Garbage

We live at the end of an alley that shares a driveway with the house next door. The alley is steep and narrow, with no room for parking, and it dead ends into a hillside. In the wintertime, we can get up to five hundred inches of snowfall in the mountains where we live.

There is nothing to do with the snow that falls on our driveway but shovel it down the alley. The city plow has to reverse his CAT snowplow about 200 yards until the back of the machine hits the hillside. The plow then shoves the snow all the way back down the alley and deposits it in an enormous snowbank at the end of the street.

Monday is garbage day at our house. And when we have a big snow day, we must manage the garbage. On a perfect day, it looks like this:

We put our trash out.

The neighbor puts their trash out.

We hustle outside to shovel the snow off our driveway into the alley before the snowplow arrives.

We move the neighbor's trash over to our side of the driveway.

My husband leaves the house first and drives his truck over the great big berm of snow we created so that my Subaru doesn't get stuck like last time.

The snow plow comes on time.

I rush out the front door to greet Paul, the driver, and have a friendly chit-chat about the weather, my dog, the snow, and so on.

We put the neighbor's trash back on their side of the driveway.

The garbage truck easily drives up the steep driveway without sliding backwards or getting stuck, and removes the garbage.

An hour later, it returns to take out our neighbor's garbage, because the garbage lift is only on one side of the truck.

We bring our cans back inside our garage.

We deliver our neighbor's cans back to their garage so that my husband has room to maneuver his truck into the garage when he comes home.

If any of these events don't happen on time or in the right order, it causes a bottleneck. The snow mounts and piles into a mountain in our driveway. We either get trapped inside our house, or stuck parking many blocks away from our house, since we can't park on the street in the winter because of the snowplow.

I know, "first world problems," right? However, I'm not complaining. I'm simply painting a picture of what management looks like to me. Constant vigilance, effort, control, and a large expenditure of energy and time.

Before my understanding of the Three Principles, I felt like I was constantly managing my experience of life the way I managed my driveway. I spent a lot of time sifting through the content of my thoughts, wondering why I thought the way that I did. I analyzed what a thought meant about me. I moved an unhelpful thought over here, and placed a positive thought over there.

I rearranged the circumstances of my outside world to prevent certain thoughts from coming into my internal world. I avoided certain situations — networking events, parties, the dentist's office — in the outside world in order to avoid a certain feeling.

I see now that thoughts are like snowflakes. The weight of a snowflake by itself is really nothing at all. But if enough snowflakes pile together on a thin tree branch, the branch will bend and break under the weight.

Similarly, one thought by itself is pretty light. But if we pack enough thoughts together — by continuing to focus our attention on them and how important they are — suddenly we have a pretty substantial snowball. A million thoughts on our mind. It's time to call the snowplow!

The inside-out nature of the mind helps us see all the unnecessary thinking we carry. Because the content of our thinking is irrelevant, we can stop lugging it around.

Remember, too, that it is not necessary to analyze our thinking before we let it go. Many people ask me how to let go of their negative thinking. They want to analyze it and know why they have it, where it came from. But do you analyze the contents of your kitchen trash before you throw it away? No! You recognize that it's garbage and you throw it out. Without fanfare, without a parade.

Much of our personal thinking is garbage. We can identify it as garbage by its feel. If it feels heavy, tight, or out of control, it's probably not helping. And in tossing out the refuse of our thinking, we create space to be in our natural state. Contrary to what it may seem, the opposite of a busy mind is not boredom, apathy or becoming a couch potato.

Our natural state is one of calm and contented action. We are able to see clearly what the next right step is in the direction we are heading. We still cannot see forty-nine steps ahead. But we can take one wise step at a time from present-moment awareness. Just like the weather system that brings the snow and the sun, there is a natural flow to our emotional weather system. We don't have to manage our internal storms as much as we think we do. Our system resets on its own without us.

Kindness of the Design

"You are the infinite creative potential of the entire f*cking universe… deal with it."

— Michael Neill

Most people are comfortable with the explanation that nature is intelligent. Year after year, plants grow from seeds, forests rejuvenate after a fire, and children transform into teenagers with facial hair. Human bodies grow babies, heal injuries, digest food for energy, and quietly engage in a thousand other biological processes that we can't even see.

Something within us—but also beyond us—is making that happen. Most people have witnessed the intelligence of life in some form or another: the incredible, miraculous process of life in the pursuit of life.

The proof of an innate intelligence in life is all around us, yet when it comes to our own mental health there is a general feeling of broken-ness. So many people are searching for happiness and can't find it, and end up dealing with stress, anxiety, or depression. When we feel some of these lower emotions, we suffer through the discomfort. We feel like we have to fix it, figure it out, or take some action to create the higher feelings of happiness or peace.

Yet, we would never feel like we had to *force* our body to digest a slice of pizza. We feed ourselves the delicious pizza and the body innately knows what to do with it.

Similarly, we have innate mental health that is always working for us; we just don't see it that way. **Low feelings are *not* a sign that the system is broken.** Low moods tell us that our mental health is working just the way it is supposed to. What many consider **"negative feelings" are part of the intelligence of the design**. They are simply the clues that kindly tell us that our awareness is currently in a head full of clouds.

When we get a cold or a flu, it's actually our immune system doing its job to keep us physically healthy. It detects a virus or bacteria, and it produces mucus, phlegm or a high fever to help purge the body of the invader. When we're lying in bed binge-watching *Ozark*, it appears that we are broken. However, our illness is actually a sign that our immune system is healthy, active, and vital.

The same is true for our mental health. If we are able to maintain some objectivity around our thoughts, we might be able to see that our negative thoughts are actually trying to keep us healthy. A low mood alerts us to the fact that we have drifted away from our natural state of peace and ease. Our feelings give us information about how many clouds are passing across our blue sky.

When we recognize this, our inner dialogue begins to shift. Instead of analyzing, diagnosing, running away from or trying to fix our sad thoughts, we begin to see them with distance and clarity. *Oh, I'm having really sad thoughts today. The sad thoughts don't mean anything about me other than that I'm a human being experiencing sad thoughts.*

I used to be an expert at managing my feelings. I had every tool and technique under the sun to help me manage my overwhelming thoughts.

I should go for a run.

I can't eat that salad because there's gluten in the dressing.

I need a new hairstyle.

When it looks to us like life is a battle that needs to be fought, or an overwhelming situation to control, or something that needs to be better, then using our tools make perfect sense. Tools are great for fixing.

However, when we begin to look at negative feelings as part of the beauty of our design, we no longer see our experience as something that has to be managed. We are less tempted by the effortful and ultimately unrealistic task of managing our experience in pursuit of well-being.

We can set down our tools and learn to truly accept, because no matter what we are feeling, we are always well. **Well-being is innate**. Our thoughts simply obscure that fact.

It comes down to trust. Can we trust that setting down our thoughts will allow the innate intelligence of life to move through us?

Look to nature for inspiration, to remember the intelligence of the design. Trees lose their leaves in the fall and bloom again in the spring. Sea turtles are able to navigate back to the exact beach where they buried their last clutch of eggs three or four years earlier. The pull of the Moon's gravity on the Earth is what holds our planet in place.

We are built to thrive. Just as we go to sleep and wake up, as night balances day, and as trees shed their leaves only to bloom again, our negative emotions are part of the design. They are there not to convey meaning, but simply to wake us up to the true reality of our present moment. **We are not broken.** We are part of the whole, complete, and perfect intelligence of the entire f*cking universe.

Relieved for a Disease

I woke up, blinked my eyes and stared at the ceiling, which appeared to be sliding at a severe slant away from me.

Oh shit, I thought. *Not again. Please no, please no.* I gingerly sat up in bed and was greeted by a wave of nausea as my feet hit the floor. I crawled to the bathroom to begin my thirty-six hour shift of projectile vomiting.

Nope, not pregnant. Vertigo.

For the past five years, I have experienced episodes of severe vertigo that sneak attack with no warning. I feel great in the evening. Then, *BAM!* I wake up in the morning and the whole world is flipped on its axis. I can't get out of bed, walk to the bathroom, or even turn my head to the side without severe nausea and vomiting.

The first time it happened I developed a ringing in my ears called tinnitus that never went away. I hated my tinnitus and tried every remedy I could Google in order to fix it. The constant ringing ruined my meditation practice and wreaked havoc with my sleep. Never finding a cure, I eventually became accustomed to the low frequency hum; it was like getting used to the incessant ticking of an analog clock in the living room.

Eventually, after four years of managing these unexpected and unexplained attacks, I was diagnosed with Meniere's Disease. It's a condition where fluid builds up in the inner ear, causing dysfunction to the vestibular system. *I wasn't going crazy!* I've never been so excited to have a disease in my life. I literally skipped out of the hospital, elated with the good news.

Apparently I *did* receive warnings about imminent vertigo attacks; they were just disguised as irritating symptoms. Yup, it was the tinnitus. The very thing I loathed for so long was actually trying to help me. When the fluid started to build up in my inner ear, the ringing in my ears got louder. My body was giving me helpful information the whole time. I was just ignoring it because I found it irritating.

Unfortunately we don't get to choose the way in which our body tells us what we need to know, which can feel uncomfortable.

Now I know that when my tinnitus grows louder, it means that the fluid in my body is increasing. It is a warning sign that I have to be more strict about my diet (Meneire's is often triggered by sodium, caffeine, alcohol, and tobacco--in other words, anything fun). If I ignore what my body is trying to tell me, I'm much more likely to have an attack of vertigo.

Our bodies are innately intelligent. This is true when it comes to our mental health as well. We can use our negative feelings as information. Instead of railing against having a negative feeling, as I did with my tinnitus, we can see that negative feelings are alerting us to our current state of mind. They are telling us that we are caught up in a whole mess of thinking.

When I eat too much salt, my ears ring. This lets me know that I've eaten too much salt. When I worry too much, I experience the feeling of anxiety. This lets me know that I've been worrying too much.

The thoughts and feelings might be uncomfortable or irritating, but they are letting us know that we are caught up in clouds of thought. With this awareness, we can relax in the knowledge that the feelings will pass on their own. Eventually, we will hear and feel the quiet once again.

Fear is Working For Us

The weather was stunning, the kind of September day in Colorado that feels like a gift, one made even more precious by its impermanence. I was paddle boarding on Stagecoach Lake. The lake is not huge in comparison to other reservoirs, or by Great Lake standards. However, it is big enough that when I stood alone on a ten foot paddle board in the middle of it, I felt very small.

I drifted on the board as boats motored past and the wind swept by, breathing in the clouds and the tall grasses, feeling contentment and peace wash over me. Then I had an interesting thought: *If I didn't know how to swim, I would be terrified right now.*

It struck me that the simple fact of understanding that I could swim, and also that I was wearing a PFD (personal floatation device), allowed me to feel safe and content. If I didn't know those things, I realized I would be having an entirely different experience on the board—most likely one filled with panic, anxiety, worry, doubt and fear.

I've worked with several clients who were exhausted by their own anxious thoughts. Habitually experiencing fear or anxiety can make a person feel very small, like they are drifting all alone on a very small paddle board in the middle of a very large lake.

There was a time when I was terrified of my own fear, when I did not realize that there was a deeper feeling underneath my thinking, a space within that quietly guides me back home. Without that knowledge my fears appeared very real and quite scary. Kind of like being stuck in the middle of a lake and not knowing how to swim.

There is a space within all of us that feels like home. It lies just underneath the chattery surface of our current thinking. Because we are always feeling our thinking, we can use our feelings as navigational tools.

We can use the insecure feelings as a sign that we have drifted away from our center. When we feel fear, worry, or doubt, it is **not** a cue to investigate the "why" behind those feelings. It is simply a sign that we have drifted away from shore into our personal thinking, and away from our inner wisdom.

There is a homeostatic setting for our thinking; it wants to level out at a reasonable volume. No matter the challenges we are facing, there is a place underneath where we can feel grounded even when our head is spinning. We just have to remember that it is there, and let it naturally reset us.

We instinctively know this. When a child in our care gets hurt, we tell them to take three big breaths, or we kiss their booboo to make it feel better. These actions help them reset. As adults, we know it's time to take a vacation when we are over-stressed. When we return, our thinking has settled (hopefully!).

When we begin to see our thoughts as ripples on the surface of a lake, we can rest in the knowing that there is a deeper mind in the water below. There is peace, calm and contentment the farther we go below the surface of our personal thinking.

Knowing this is similar to knowing that I can swim when I'm alone on a tiny paddle board in the middle of a large lake.

Recognizing that wisdom is always there for me underneath the surface of my thinking is like wearing a PFD when the water of our life gets rough. No matter how choppy the water gets, I know that I will stay afloat.

Shattering the Glass

"Thought creates our world and then says, 'I didn't do it.'"

— David Bohm

Last spring, there was a female pileated woodpecker nesting in a dead tree just outside our kitchen window. For about a week, she tapped on our window incessantly, knocking and pecking for about five minutes straight. Then she would fly back to her nest to take a short rest. *Perhaps to grab some Gatorade?* After that she would return to the window, tap-tap-tapping away. It seemed like exhausting work.

Apparently, the woodpecker was living under the premise that if she just tapped on that glass one more freaking time, she might get the something inside our house that she so desperately wanted. *Was it the little red figurine in the windowsill? The glass jar holding wine corks? Did she need to tell me a secret?* We didn't know. We cleaned everything that the woodpecker could possibly want off the kitchen counters. And still she came; still she tapped.

Though this relentless woodpecker's behavior seemed fruitless to us, we humans often behave in similar ways. We transform the flowing energy of thought into solid concepts that hold thought in place. We innocently create walls of glass — our versions of success, failure, career, or balance — with our thinking. Then, we tap on these walls incessantly, wondering why we can't break through the glass.

We end up having a lot of thinking about concepts, and it stresses us out. So we decide to have better and more positive thinking about the concept. But we forget that the concept itself is made of thought.

The trick of thought is that it doesn't look like thought. It looks like truth.

I once worked with a client who had innocently created a concept called "success" that was based on the premise that it required hard work and sacrifice. What that looked like on the surface was working sixty hours a week, preparing every meal for her family of four, and running at least seven miles a day.

She was spending a lot of brainpower thinking about all the time she didn't have to share with her family, adding feelings of guilt, selfishness and blame to an already full plate. She was exhausted and burnt out from tap-tap-tapping on the glass of success. The good news was that those feelings were letting her know that she was running up against a glass wall of her own thinking. By seeing that she had more possibility around what success could feel like — fun, easy, and abundant — she shattered the glass and enjoyed life a whole lot more.

We believe our thought-created concepts are true, and we forget that we made them up in the first place. We live inside the glass walls of our premises, thinking that those walls are solid. But the walls are made of smoke. When we are operating unknowingly under a thought-created concept, we're acting like the woodpecker tapping on a window, expecting to get into the house.

The solution is simple: see the glass.

There is nothing to do but *notice*. The noticing of a thought is the beginning of its undoing. It frees us up to start looking in different directions, to stop tapping on the glass, to find new ways inside.

Double Parked

"The meaning of life is just to be alive. It is so plain and so obvious and so simple, and yet everybody rushes around in a great panic as if it were necessary to achieve something beyond themselves."

— Alan Watts

As the youngest of five children, I was always last, hustling to catch up with my bigger, faster, and cooler older brother and sisters.

Once, we were travelling through a train station which had one of those circular revolving doors; when you went through it was like stepping into a fraction of a revolving pizza pie. I was desperate to fit into the same triangular stall as my big brother, but I arrived a second too late. My body made it halfway in and my face got squeezed between the glass door and the wall.

I was too slow. I got stuck.

As an adult, I had a sense of urgency that permeated the background of my thinking. A constant soundtrack playing on low volume throughout my day that sped me up and created the illusion that there was never enough time. I rushed to yoga, hustled to get the grocery shopping done, hurried through every task at work to get to the next thing...

I once heard one of my teachers, George Pransky, say that he noticed he was living at a pace as if he was always "double parked." I felt the exact same way. A subtle, low hum of "hurry up, hurry up, don't get stuck" played on repeat in the background of my mind.

This sense of urgency had pervaded my life to where I always felt behind and "not enough." I was hurtling through life to achieve more, to be more productive, to catch up with others (whoever *they* were). And when my world looked outside-in, it made sense that happiness came from doing more stuff, faster and with greater efficiency.

Now I see that there is nowhere to get to. I am already here.

This insight did not come like a hammer — more like a nail file just gently scraping away at my false perception of "not enough time," one millimeter at a time.

I continue to catch myself in this particular train of thought nearly every day, especially when writing this book. *Oh my god, it's taking so long! Why am I so slow? I've been writing this forevvvvvvver. This should have been done months ago! I'm quitting.*

The truth is that writing a book, building a business, raising a family, or finding our life's work *takes the time that it takes*. No more and no less.

Now I see that my sense of urgency is a clue that I'm stuck in thought. Any time I start to feel that old familiar rushing sensation, or that something needs to happen, like, *yesterday*, or that I have stopped breathing... I pause.

I stop chasing the imaginary tail of productivity. I rest, catch my breath, and fall back into the present state of mind. When I stop thinking about writing and actually write, it's astounding the amount of words that magically appear on the screen.

Most of us know, intellectually, that time is a thought-created construct, but it can feel so viscerally real. It takes some time to recalibrate to a slowed-down mind. The reward is the feeling of spaciousness that comes from living in the right now. By clearing out more white space in my mind, there is much more room for creativity to arrive.

Tree Therapy

"What will be left of all the fear and wanting associated with your problematic life situation that every day takes up most of your attention? A dash — one or two inches long, between the date of birth and the date of death on your gravestone."

— Eckhart Tolle

It's fall in the Rocky mountains, which basically consists of the month of October. It is a short and beautiful burst of color before six months of snow blankets the world in white. Most of the trees have already lost their leaves, preparing for the plummet in temperatures to come.

Without any context of the cycle of seasons, it would appear that something is wrong with a tree that's gone barren in preparation for winter. Its berries are shriveled on the vine. Its leaves are either dead or gone. Its branches are dull and lifeless. If we took one of these barren trees to tree therapy, the tree would be diagnosed as unwell.

Perhaps the tree is depressed or lonely or sad? Maybe we need to fix the tree? I know! Let's Botox some plumpness back into the berries, glue its leaves back on, and paint the branches a brighter stain of brown.

This might sound absurd. However, it is what we do to ourselves when we don't understand the workings of our mind. Much like the seasons, we have moods and experiences that fluctuate over time, going up and down, reaching high and dipping low. When we are in a low mood, we take a snapshot of ourselves in that mood and diagnose ourselves with a problem.

We spend so much mental energy on what is wrong that we completely miss what is right. We overly attend to what is broken and try to mend, replace, or repair our parts. But in doing this we miss the full cycle of our experience. With a little time and patience, we will eventually feel better. We heal on our own by design.

We are feeling creatures. And our feelings change moment to moment, day to day, month to month, year to year. If we can relax into this natural rhythm of experience we expend so much less mental energy trying to fix ourselves in autumn when our leaves fall off. We get to be as a tree and live through the full spectrum of experience, knowing that no matter what season it is, we are healthy and alive. Spring is just around the corner.

Dowsing the Well

Every human being is searching for the feeling of well-being that is our true nature. We are like dowsing rods constantly searching for the presence of water to quench our thirst. And we are unknowingly standing in the middle of a deep well.

Sometimes the way in which we go about feeling better looks inappropriate or dysfunctional to other people. For example, it can appear to the outside observer to be laziness, resistance, or even addictive behavior. This sheds a new light on why people may behave in seemingly strange ways.

What if heroin users, video game addicts, and agoraphobics are all just trying to feel better? It may be that their addictive or irrational behavior is the only method they've found so far that works for settling their mind. If it truly looks to me like I cannot feel well until I have a hit of a cigarette, then I'll keep smoking. If it truly looks like being in a public place makes me have a panic attack, then I will never leave the safety and comfort of home.

In an outside-in world, we have to change our circumstance to change a feeling. In an inside-out world, we realize that all we have to know is that the feeling is coming from thought—and let it pass.

Seeing people as innately well no matter their behavior flips the script on how we see and handle challenging behavior situations. I once coached a client who was struggling with her nine-year-old — who was refusing to do her homework and was spending what her mom thought was "way too much time" on the iPad.

My client was looking for solutions to the perceived problem that her daughter was being obstinate, difficult, and downright lazy. When we discussed the radical notion that her daughter's wisdom might actually be guiding her to feel better, a different question came forward: *How could spending hours on the iPad be the solution for her daughter to feel better?*

And then we stumbled upon a reasonable answer. My client wondered if her daughter was creating stressful and pressured thinking around getting her homework done. If it appeared to her daughter that the stress was truly coming from the homework, and not her thoughts, then it seemed natural that she would avoid doing her homework in favor of the iPad.

Our wisdom is always guiding us to feel better. Knowing this, when we look at the things we're trying to avoid we can also become aware of the thinking we're having around them.

There is a reservoir of resilience and a well of being within us that can be dowsed at any time. Every human being longs to feel their wellness. Coincidentally, every human being on the planet is already well. They just don't know it.

Invitation to Reader

What does it mean if your bad feelings or low moods are actually helping you?

What are all the ways in which you see the beauty and intelligence of nature? Of the human body?

If you are already designed perfectly, what can you let yourself stop doing or believing?

Part Five: Of Clouds + Sky

"We have the most wonderful job in the world. We find people in various stages of sleep. And then we get to tap them on the shoulder and be with them as they wake up to the full magnificence of life."

— Sydney Banks

Reconnecting with God

There was one rather large story that I had been innocently breathing life into for as long as I could remember. It wore many different costumes over the years, going through many rewrites and rough drafts.

It was my story around God.

The image behind the word "God" has evolved for me over time. When I was little, God was a much larger, more bearded version of my Dad. He lived in a luxury apartment somewhere above me. He was definitely a "He" and was a mix between Superman and Santa Claus who was also all-knowing, all-seeing, and could fly.

Being a good little Catholic I prayed every night, reciting my memorized prayers to the angels and all the saints—especially Saint Anthony, the finder of lost things.

I volunteered. I was kind to all. I stood up for the underdog. I shopped at thrift stores. I took Communion. I confessed. I cared. A lot.

In high school, as I grappled with the death of young classmates, I confided in a priest. While I was pouring out my sadness and grief, the priest fell asleep. This happened with two separate priests! I had turned to them in desperation, and they fell asleep.

I understand now that priests are only human. But those moments were what turned me away from the church, and I haven't really been back since.

But *church* is not *God*.

I still believed in something.

Then in my early twenties, my cousin, PJ, died far too young from a drug overdose. My faith in something "higher" started to slowly deteriorate. I didn't blame God, but I certainly didn't think it served any purpose to believe in the big guy upstairs anymore.

Shit just happens. People die. They don't come back to visit you as angels. They don't whisper guidance about life into your ear. Their ghost does not appear to you in the kitchen when you call them forth. Life just is, and there is no meaning behind anything.

So I lost my faith. I lost it hard. Too cynical even for atheism, I labeled myself a nihilist. I believed in nothing.

I was all on my own. I felt separate from everyone and everything.

Eventually I turned to running and exercise to manage my sadness. I changed my diet, drank less alcohol, cut back on sugar, and eliminated gluten. These changes had a huge impact on my body and my mood. I started to feel better.

Soon I was a full-on convert to the church of *Eat Right and Exercise and You Shall be Saved*. I definitely went all preachy and shit. But finally, I felt, I had found something to believe in that yielded physical and tangible results. I ran ultra-marathons on trails, in the woods, in the twilight, with soft rain falling on my shoulders. This became my new church, my new form of worship.

My soul began to knit itself back together again. Nothing made me feel more connected to the Universe, to God, to the Infinite than being outside for long periods of time in the sanctity of the woods. And as a result I began to open myself back up to the potential of God.

It was through practicing yoga that I was first introduced to the non-dualistic belief that we are not separate from God. That we are one and the same. I became aware of a new language to describe what I had always felt, that God was somehow inside of me. Not a separate, superhuman in a human form who hovered above me, but an energy that lived *through* me.

Everything clicked when I found the Three Principles. This understanding felt true, and it did not have any dogma or rules attached to it. The Three Principles are not a prescription for how to live life. They merely describe how our mind works to create the illusion that we are separate from the intelligence of life.

All of the thinking, the judging, the running, and the wondering *about* God blocked me from feeling God, from trusting that there was something larger than me at work. When I finally was able to see that my story around God was what was preventing me from experiencing God, everything shifted.

Reconnecting with the God of my own understanding felt like returning home to myself after years of searching for the answer outside of me. The answer was here all along, quietly hidden in the space within me, within every single one of us.

Spiritual Roommates

During my freshman year of college, I shared a tiny dorm room with an awesome human named Carla. We shared such a small space that by the end of freshman year we were finishing each other's sentences and laughing at each other's corny jokes. The tight quarters created a unique blend of our personalities. My aunt nicknamed us Sarla, a witty combination of Sarah and Carla. I vividly remember returning back to our dorm room one night after stuffing my face full of fried food at dinner. When I opened the door Carla exclaimed, "Oh, thank God you're back, I'm starving!" I replied without thinking, "You can't be starving, I just ate!"

We have within us two similar, seemingly inseparable roommates, the Thinker and the Watcher. In fact, they are not really two distinct entities, but two ways in which we are able to use Mind. The Thinker uses Mind to think about ourselves. It is the story-weaver and believer. The Watcher, on the other hand, is the witness to our experience.

Most of us tend to live in the clouds, thinking our thoughts, forgetting entirely about watching from our being-ness, the blue sky. And when we live as the Thinker, our thoughts can easily weigh us down because they feel so significant, real and true.

The meeting tomorrow will be a disaster.

I'll never get that promotion.

I'm such a loser.

There is no space for blue sky to appear behind the clouds and remind us that we are more than our thoughts.

So the Thinker forgets it's part of something much bigger, that it could not exist without the blue sky to float through. Awareness is infinite. With practice in developing our own awareness, we begin to create space between our thinking and our being.

And, in the space between is quiet.

We are not who we think we are. We are that which experiences thought.

Maybe I'm not shy, I just think I am.

Maybe I do know the answer, I just think I don't.

Maybe I'm the full potential of the universe, I just think I'm not.

The more we identify with our observing self, our Watcher, the less we identify with—and get trapped in—the state of the Thinker. When we are not reacting to our thoughts as if they are real, we're able to simply observe them.

As my Watcher becomes more and more removed from my Thinker, I find my thinking self to be hilarious! *That's so cute that you think that your age is relevant to getting this job.* Now I know that all of my thoughts are *just* thoughts drifting in and out of my awareness. No one thought is any more real than another.

My Watcher is very loving. She sees my thinking as a condition of being human and not as one of being inferior or inept. She smiles at me in the way that a parent smiles at a stumbling toddler just learning to walk. The parent knows that the child will eventually get it, and that there's a learning curve. We're giving them space to learn on their own.

That is what spirituality means to me: creating space in between the thinking self and the observing self. Creating space for breath, for possibility, for love, to be inspired and lit up by this incredibly human existence. It doesn't have to be serious, it can be fun and loving and real. It requires both distance and surrender.

Our awareness connects us to the bigger part of ourselves. The Watcher has the ability to become aware of our thinking and distance itself from it. That's how we know that the thinking self and the observing self are separate. If they were one and the same, the Watcher would not be able to be aware of itself.

My Watcher notices, without judgment, as my thinking passes. Without getting involved in my thinking, with pure curiosity and sometimes even amusement, I observe. Becoming a spiritual person is a practice in creating a cushion between the Thinker and the Watcher. They are like spiritual roommates, who get along best when there's a little space between them.

Infinite Doorways

My biggest struggle as a young person was making decisions. Growing up as the youngest of five children, I was able to coast through most challenges with other people making decisions for me. I believed I didn't know how to make a decision for myself. I changed my major in college seven times, switched schools twice, and regretfully bailed from a study abroad program in Spain.

I innocently created an imaginary destination where my future success and happiness resided. It looked to me like every doorway into this fantasy room opened onto either life or death, black or white. There was one right way and one wrong way, and that was it. If I studied psychology I could never be a radio DJ. I could study education, but what if I hated it? I was paralyzed by fear that if I didn't find the one and only right way, I would end up miserable.

The inside-out understanding helped me to see that there is no right answer for how to live life. If my experience of my life is always being filtered through my thought, that means if I try something out and I "fail," that feeling of failure is only coming from my thoughts. I no longer have to avoid a feeling, because I know it's temporary.

Life then becomes one big game asking to be played. The game of starting a business, training for a marathon, writing a book, asking for a raise, or starting a family. I will be okay no matter what game I play, regardless of win or lose.

There is not a real, tangible thing called "failure." There is no piano dropping from the ceiling if I get it wrong. We create the concept of failure out of our thoughts and behave as if it were real. We forget that we made up the concept of failure in the first place.

And we not only make up failure—we make up what failure means about us.

If I fail, then I'm not smart.

If he doesn't like me, then I am not pretty enough.

If I don't get the job, I'm unemployable.

That's all made up.

At the same time, there is no door that leads to a utopic fantasyland where everything works out perfectly. Just like failure, "perfect" is a thought-created illusion of the mind. Behind any door is love and loss, joy and pain, wisdom and illusion.

Still... It seems to us that there must really be a room where peace, contentment, and joy live. And it feels like the only way out of our feelings of stress, anxiety and worry is to find that room. We know the room is there because we've felt it before when we did a certain activity. So we think that that activity is the only doorway into the room. We crave the room. We strive for the room. We effort to enter the room. We cry, "I need the f*cking room!"

But the way into the room is to see that the room is an illusion. The illusion is created by two gifts of the human experience—thought and consciousness—through a process that happens so fast that we don't see the process behind it.

We have a thought. Our consciousness lights up that thought and brings it to life. It brings it to life using a whole crew of special effects experts. We feel the thought—it has texture and sound and a pulse. The thought is alive. It is so alive that it feels like our reality.

But really it's just a thought. And it obscures our sense of the third gift of the human experience: our innate well-being. Our natural setting of peace, joy, and contentment. That inner space is as vast as the ocean, the sky, or the milky way. It is infinite and expansive. Acting as if it can possibly be contained in a tiny room is like trying to cage a lion in a milk carton.

There is no one right answer, correct path, or magic choice that will lead me to definitive happiness. Since happiness is an inside job, any door we choose is equally able to bring contentment and joy as well as struggles and challenges. Since every door is an equal opportunity of experience, why not choose the thing that lights us up, that makes us feel giddy, or even that scares us a little?

We are sitting, standing, and living in the middle of this good feeling all the time. Not sometimes — *always*.

Nobody is wiser about your own life than you. You get to choose whichever door feels right to you in the moment. You actually can't get it wrong.

Instead of striving, efforting, stressing, or shaming ourselves for not being in the room, we can relax. Just like in *The Matrix*, there is no spoon. There is no room. We are standing right in the middle of it. We are already here.

Falling into Presence

Everything we seek is actually already here in the blue sky of our being. Clarity, creativity, confidence, contentment, peace, and fulfillment: it's all right here, waiting for us just behind the clouds of our thinking. In the ever present moment of Now.

It is not something out there in the future, or something *that asshole* took from us, or something that would have happened if only the stars had aligned perfectly in the past. We don't magically obtain it when we score the right career, have the proper amount of digits in the bank account, or finally get some down time.

We may taste it in these fleeting moments, but not because of the circumstance. It's because when we achieve our goals, the swirl of thinking about those goals slows down, and our minds naturally settle.

The Now is (unsurprisingly) available to us in every single moment. It is not a low-stock, "get it while you can" item in the grocery store, like trying to score milk in the middle of a snowstorm. It's more like the limitless supply of gum at the checkout aisle, an infinite "buy-one-get-free" field of awareness.

In the *now*, we are always ready, always at our very best. Unencumbered by the thought-created illusion that we aren't good enough, smart enough or whatever enough. In the *now*, we are always at our highest potential. We are whole, complete and perfect just as we are. When we rest in the present moment, we get a tiny taste of that enormous concept called enlightenment.

The word "enlightenment" has gotten a lot of attention over the years. And the way we use the lofty word makes it seem like enlightenment is a goal to be reached, or something that can be attained and sustained for a lifetime.

But I think enlightenment simply means "to feel lighter." When we are unburdened by our heavy thinking we feel lighter, or enlightened, even if only for a split second. We don't have to be monks or do a thousand incantations or perform miracles. We fall out of thinking and into the space of lightness that is right now. We fall into presence.

What if the big secret of life is that there is nowhere to get to?

The great mystery lies in the miracle that we are all here and existing. That's it. Just by being alive, we are already living out our purpose: to live.

We have already arrived. There is no further destination beyond right here. We made it! That means that anything else we achieve on top of our existence is icing on the cake. Anything that sounds interesting to you or sparks a little light of excitement—that's the feeling to follow. We get to navigate by joy on this rollercoaster ride of life.

Wisdom Spotting

There is an intelligence to our design. The same stuff that animates us also animates the birds, the trees, and the octopus. There is a divine intelligence that ensures that buds become blossoms, acorns grow into oak trees, and tadpoles turn into frogs. The seasons cycle every year and the ocean tides rise and fall every day.

The word that resonates most strongly with me in an attempt to point to this universal intelligence of life, or god-energy, is the word "wisdom."

We don't "have" wisdom. We ARE wisdom.

Wisdom is not something to attain or achieve. It is something that has been operating for us, in us, our entire life. Wisdom does not float down from the clouds riding a chariot with rainbow wheels that's pulled by a unicorn (although that would be amazing).

Wisdom often just appears as common sense.

I'm going to make a doctor's appointment.

It's time to ask for a raise.

I'm going to give up drinking for a month.

I need to hire a professional.

These are all examples of wisdom working for us—giving us

the knowing we need in the moment that we need it.

Noticing wisdom is a practice in noticing when we *know*.

It is noticing when our mind is telling us to reset to our natural state of well-being, even when it doesn't look like it. Any time we slow down and take a break — that's usually our wisdom showing up. *Not exercising for a day? Eating a pint of ice cream? Taking a week off social media?* Wisdom! For reals.

When I first started coaching full time, I put an immense amount of pressure on myself to write dazzling blogs, post daily on social media and fill my calendar with coaching sessions. My mind was inundated with pressurized thinking and, as a result, I experienced an intense lack of motivation and an excess of procrastination.

So what did I do? I picked up my guitar and just played music instead of working. I allowed myself to not do anything, even when my intellect wanted to chime in about how lazy I was being.

And you know what?

With a clearer mind, I suddenly had loads of inspiring ideas about what I wanted to write and create. At the time, playing the guitar just seemed like the only appealing item on the menu. Only in hindsight could I see that it was my wisdom at work.

Our culture demands speed and consumption. Our cultural conditioning will constantly tell us to speed up and do more doing when really the answer often lies in the opposite direction. My wisdom guided me to a place of a settled mind so that I could see clearly how I wanted to naturally move forward.

Our mind is searching for the feeling of home — it just doesn't always appear that way. The more we can notice when we are out of balance, the faster we come home to solid ground. We become aware of our natural tendency to restore. With a more quiet mind, we have clearer ideas about what we need. We notice that the obvious answer has been there all along.

There is an intelligence to our design that somehow gives us the wisdom and knowledge we seek in the moment that we need it. If you commit to holding a high level of attention to noticing your own wisdom, you will improve. It's so simple. Notice wisdom more, and you will feel connected to it more of the time. Look for wisdom and you will see it clearly operating in your life every day.

Play Like an Otter

It was a crisp fall day. The sun sparkled on the water as I strolled over the pedestrian bridge crossing the meandering river. I looked down and saw an otter floating on his back, his gaze directed right at me. I swear he was smiling. The otter did a quick flick of his body, splashing and circling a few times, then dove back under the water.

According to my spirit animal book, otters bring a sense of playfulness and fun into life. Just as I noticed the otter in the river, I had been very seriously considering my coaching business— planning and mapping and strategizing. It was tight and very un-fun thinking. I believe the otter was reminding me to play.

We have a tendency to make everything so serious. Getting a certain amount of "likes" on social media means that I am popular. Nailing *Bird of Paradise* pose in yoga class means that I'm a good yogi. Getting this job means I'm a worthy human.

"This" means "that" about me.

There is a liberation when we strip away the meaning we assign to things. For example, when writing isn't about what a smart and intellectual person I am, it is just something I enjoy doing. When the job I have means nothing about my character, I'm free to choose any job that pays the bills or sounds fun.

We make up the meaning of the events in our lives. The work of life is to realize we created that meaning — that we are, in fact, creating all the time. We are born creators. Creating our experience from thoughts.

Thought creates walls and invisible boundaries and barriers that seem real. *I'm stuck in this job, in this relationship, in this mood.*

But we are never really stuck. It only takes seeing the wall of thought. And that moment of awareness — *Hey, I created that wall from thought!* — is often enough to tear the wall down.

As I watched the otter twirl and play in the water, I wondered if there was an evolutionary reason for its sense of play? If an otter had to be employed, I wonder what he would be? Probably a circus clown, or a stand-up comedian. Maybe a paragliding instructor.

Perhaps living with a sense of playfulness simply releases good feelings in the otter, just like it does in humans. When we are playing and having fun, life just seems to go better.

Watch children for five minutes and you will witness our innate sense of play. It is in our true nature to be playful and filled with joy.

Joy is the unburdened feeling of not being weighed down by our habitual thinking. The patterns and habits and spinning thoughts that wrap and tangle, making us feel tight, disconnected, lost.

When we feel our thoughts of anger, sadness, and worry, it appears as if our joy is gone. But really it's just obscured by the thinking that rests on top of it. The joy is always there, waiting for you to rediscover it. Waiting for you to drop out of whatever it is you're so concerned about and back into the playfulness of life.

When We Stop Searching

There seems to be a universal truth: the moment we stop frantically searching for something, we find it again.

Lost keys, sunglasses, Hydroflask . . . whatever it is. When we stop looking for it, it magically reappears.

I confirmed this truth by conducting a detailed scientific study...Well, okay, by casually interviewing coaching clients, coworkers, and friends. Without fail, when I shared my hypothesis, they all said, "Yes!"

One interviewee exclaimed, "I looked everywhere for my reading glasses and they were sitting on my head."

A coworker revealed, "I had to take the bus to work because I couldn't find my car keys. When I returned home, I found them in the ignition."

Another commented, "I looked everywhere for my book and when I gave up I found it sitting on the coffee table in plain sight."

So, yes, given this, ahem, thoroughly researched scientific study, it appears to be a universal truth.

More importantly, this phenomenon points to a real truth: that there is an intelligence to life just underneath the surface of our perceived control (or lack of it) over things. When I am in grasping or gripping mode—whether it's looking for my keys or trying to figure out my career—I am blocking the natural flow of life.

I once had a conversation with a doctor of osteopathy about life and spirituality. She told me that we are all born with some slack in our rope. As life lives through us and we suffer injury or trauma, it takes a little bit of the slack out. The rope becomes so stretched and taut, that the smallest bend snaps it.

I believe we do this with our thinking, too. We think we can out-think our problem, so we think some more and some more. We habitually think about our thinking, and as we do the slack in the line gets tighter and tighter. Until there is no slack left and the line snaps.

As human beings, we think. Our thinking creates the experience of how our life feels to us in any given moment. We are constantly feeling the experience of our thinking and not the feeling of an absolute external reality.

We think all day long—high thoughts, low thoughts, boring thoughts, interesting thoughts. Our thoughts are transient. We tend to pick up on certain thoughts that we think are meaningful and give them more weight than necessary.

In truth, our thoughts distract us from who we really are. We allow them to run us round in circles, thinking that if we keep rifling through them we'll find the answers we're looking for.

The moment we stop searching for an answer to our life in the content of our thinking is the moment when the answer appears to us out of the blue sky. Our glasses have been sitting on the top of our head all along. Our keys are resting in the ignition.

I Walk the White Line

The desert trail meanders through cacti and over endless slickrock, coated with a thin red dust. I imagine it's a little like hiking on Mars. The slickrock trail is marked with a painted white line dashed upon the rock. While hiking over miles of continuous rock that all looks the same, it's easy to lose your way.

On a recent desert hike, I kept drifting off course, meandering my way through the red rocks and desert flowers. I had to keep coming back to the dotted white line, again and again. Wander and return, wander and return.

Coming back to our innate state of well-being is like aligning back to the white line. It is guaranteed that while wandering through life, we will get off course. We will be lured away by a new project, a new relationship, or by our thinking. It's just the nature of the terrain.

We drift away from the white line to check out a cool rock feature or a cave. It may or may not have been worth exploring. We explore and then we return.

Life is not about staying on the white line. That would be boring. It's about wandering, being curious as to what lies beyond the trail.

In order to awaken to our wisdom, it is essential that we fall asleep. It is part of the design. Sleeping and waking are a natural cycle. We drift away from our center, we fall asleep, and then we wake up and find our way again back to the white line of our true nature.

Both/And

I was in the kitchen fixing mushroom quesadillas for dinner. Because the vegetables came from one of those food delivery services, I only had the exact amount of mushrooms needed for the recipe. There were no mushrooms to spare.

My husband kept sneaking his hand onto the cutting board and stealing a mushroom slice when I wasn't looking. If I caught him, I'd playfully slap his hand away like swatting a pesky fly.

Ever since I received the news that I am unable to get pregnant, I have been struggling to allow myself to want things. Somewhere, there lingered a thought that it's not safe to want things.

I didn't even realize that I had been doing this. I noticed that each time I had a thought like, I want to make more money, I want more clients, I want to build a thriving business, I would immediately dismiss those thoughts as "just thoughts" and shut down my desires for being too egoic, selfish, or narcissistic.

Just like in the kitchen with my husband, I was slapping my own hand away when I dared to want something. Stop that. You can't have that. Not now.

In my effort to live into my spiritual nature, I was ignoring my human nature. Without realizing it, I was slapping away my own humanity. Wanting something does not make me a bad person. It just makes me a person.

It is easy to learn these principles and the amazing way we are designed and to then compartmentalize our being nature as "good" and our thinking nature as "bad." It can be tempting to create a goal to live life purely from our spiritual nature—as monastic, zen-like, floating beings that never feel anger, jealousy or irritation again.

The truth is we are both/and:

- the formless and the form
- energy and matter
- universal intelligence and personal ego
- divine goodness and bad habits
- infinite possibility and the container of our body
- creative potential and limited thinking
- loving, caring, knowing, creating and lacking, judging, planning, comparing.

We have the miraculous ability to be the mystic on the mountain bike, the rishi in the hair salon, the guru in the executive suite. We can taste a moment of lightness at the traffic light. Feel the pulse of expansion while gripping the spatula.

In the embrace of it all we find our joy, our power, our strength. I see that I am BOTH this formless, infinite, divine energy AND a formed body with thoughts, needs, and desires. We are the intersection where humanity and divinity collide. We are the beautiful mess. We are both, and. We feel the clouds of thought, and yet we are also the blue sky.

Invitation to Reader

What are ways that wisdom shows up in your life?

What does your belief in a more spiritual nature look like to you?

In what ways can you recognize that you are both clouds and sky?

How can you learn to love the beautiful mess?

Closing Poem

Did You Know?

You were born as love.
A being of light.
Even as you scream and cry and poop and vomit.
Your mind is pure. Unadulterated.
You know only what your body needs,
and you know it exactingly.
You play outside, fascinated by the world around you.
You are dazzled by lights and mirrors and bubbles.
Every bird, every grasshopper, every hum of a chainsaw
is a revelation.
As long as you are napped and fed, you are happy.
You want for nothing and enjoy every moment.
You are as the animals and trees, a wild and contented thing.
The world has not yet taught you to require more.
As you grow, your body becomes more able.
Navigating the grass nimbly with bare feet
Hopping over sprinklers and climbing under logs.
You are guided by instinct.
Your emotions are real and raw;
You have not yet learned to bury them.

Then you start learning the ways of the world.
You navigate by "should" and "ought to."

You compare, compete, and measure up to others.
You assimilate. You behave. You obey.
I am sorry.
Your pure, shiny light is covered by a layer of thinking
that says you are not perfect just as you are.
The thinking says you have to behave
in a certain way to be perfect.
That you have to work at it, effort, strive.
Become something that you are not.
Then comes another layer, and another, and another.
The golden light is buried in wrapping, layers thick.
It would take bolt cutters or a welding iron
to remove all those layers.
But the light is still there.

Did you know that you are god?
That every kiss under the bleachers,
every hand you hold,
every crush that makes your cheeks blaze pink,
every eye contact held too long,
every sly smile and awkward advance,
is the recognition of god between two people?
We are drawn in by the god in others.
We see their light and flutter to it like moths to a flame.
We are in desperate search to find our light again.
Maybe he has it, or she has it, or both.
It feels amazing when someone else sees our light
through all the layers of film and dust.
Somehow they notice
that we burn brighter from the inside out.
But we think the other person gave us our light.
We forget that it's always there.

We live in the illusion that we are separate.
We forget that we are all flavors of god.
Expressed in our own unique way.
The abundance of life is blocked by cars
and plastic and walls and glass.
Loans, bills, insurance, degrees, promotions.
Competition, comparison, social media.
We only see our own tiny slice of the world.
Everything feels scarce
Everything feels like not enough.
Yet it is god driving the Porsche,
God living in a cardboard box on the sidewalk,
God giving you a parking ticket,
God helping you pick up your groceries
that spilled down the aisle.
With every birth and death, we again see god.
The veil is lifted.
As we hold a baby and marvel at its innocence.
As we hold the hand of a loved one who has just passed.

Remember that you are god.
You are nature.
You are born whole, complete and perfect.
Your self-worth just *is*.
No need to effort or strive or seek.
Let go of the layers that have coalesced around your light.
Burn them like gossamer wings.
People need your light
to help them find their way back
to their own.

Acknowledgments

I would like to acknowledge all of the teachers and leaders in the Three Principles Community for their conviction, compassion, and courage to share what they have seen about the nature of our experience. Among my many teachers are Michael Neill, Barbara Patterson, George and Linda Pransky, Dicken Bettinger, Mavis Karn, Cathy Casey, and many others who have shared this understanding in videos, courses and books. And of course, deepest gratitude for the original messenger, Sydney Banks. Thank you all for the work you do to bring this understanding to the world so that many more people can feel a greater understanding of their own beautiful human-ness.

This book began as an incredibly rough draft that I wrote during an online course called, "Falling in Love with Writing: A Conversation in 50 chapters" with Michael Neill and Steve Chandler. The rough draft then evolved into many more drafts through another Michael Neill program, called "Creating the Impossible." That was when I chose to create, what in my mind at the time, seemed to be the impossible project of writing a bestselling book. These two courses allowed me the space and direction I needed to soldier on even when it looked truly impossible.

Many thanks to the synchronicities of life and the delightful ways that the universe places just the right people in my path at just the right time. Thanks to Niki Dean for being the first reader of an early draft and for her kind optimism and encouragement. I also found the perfect person to help bring this book fully to life in the editor and coach, Chris Nelson. Your meticulous eye for detail and ability to gently guide and steer me towards more clarity is a gift. Thank you for believing in me and in this book.

A big shout out to the staff and colleagues from the Supercoach Academy, especially my mentors Wyn Morgan, Stef Cybichowski, and Marina Galan.

Gratitude to my early readers, Stephanie Benedetto, Elsa Watson, and Meghan Muller for your encouragement and kind words.

A big group hug to my dear friends (a.k.a. *The Love Bugs*) — Kate, Amanda, Meg, and Maria — who allow for honesty, exploration, encouragement, support, spirituality, and silliness all at the same time.

Thank you to all of my coaching clients who are willing to explore the spiritual nature of life and courageously connect with their infinite potential.

Thank you to my amazing family — Mom, Dad, Jen, Beth, Dave, Andrea, Bruce, Gloria, and most especially, Tatum — you are a constant source of love and support. I am beyond grateful to have you in my life.

About the Author

Sarah Kostin is a Certified Transformative Coach and author. A former Children's Librarian, yoga teacher, web designer, and ultra-marathon runner, Sarah's love for learning, reading, and personal growth led her to an understanding of our true nature that changed her life completely. When not coaching or writing, Sarah enjoys spending time outside playing in the mountains where she lives with Team Colorado, which is comprised of her husband, her dog, and her cat. Sign up for her weekly newsletter full of articles and inspiration on how to write the next chapter of the story of your life. Learn more on her website: sarahkostin.com.

Made in United States
North Haven, CT
23 February 2022

16440166R00107